T0271329

A New Economic Anthropology

Traditionally economic anthropology has been studied by sociologists, anthropologists, and philosophers seeking to highlight the social foundations of economic action. Meanwhile, anthropological questions have remained largely untreated in economics, despite the prominence given to the individual in microeconomics. And there is very little in the way of dialogue between the two sides. This book argues for a new economic anthropology which goes beyond the conflict of economics and anthropology to show the complementarity of the two approaches. Economics needs to go beyond the stage of *homo oeconomicus* and be open to broader ideas about the person. Equally, anthropology can be enriched through the methods and models of economic theory. This new economic anthropology goes beyond a simple observation of societies. It is new because it introduces the responsible person with a wider range of characteristics, in particular vulnerability and suffering, as a subject of economics. It is a particular interpretation of economic anthropology calling for a broadening of the subject (moving from the individual to the person), range of values (admission of negative values for altruism, social capital, responsibility), and disciplinary references. Through this approach, both economics and anthropology can be enriched. This book will be of great interest to those working in the fields of economics, anthropology, philosophy, and development studies.

François Régis Mahieu is Emeritus Professor of Economics at the University of Versailles – Saint-Quentin-en-Yvelines, France. During the 1980s, he taught for eight years at the University of Abidjan, Côte d'Ivoire. He carried out numerous missions in Sub-Saharan Africa for international organizations. He is the founder of the association "Fund for Research in Economic Ethics", FREE, and scientific advisor to International Mixt Research Unit "Résiliences" (Institute of Research for Development, Paris and Ivorian Center for Economic and Social

Research, Abidjan). He has published several books to illustrate his approach, including *Altruisme. Analyses économiques* (1998), *Ethique économique, fondements anthropologiques* (2001), *Ethique économique* (2003, with Jérôme Ballet), *Responsabilité et crimes économiques* (2008), *Autour de l'anthropologie économique, actualité des écrits du Professeur André Nicolaï* (2014), and *Freedom, Responsibility and Economics of the Person* (2014).

Economics and Humanities
Series Editor: **Sebastian Berger**, *University of the West of England (UWE Bristol), UK.*

The *Economics and Humanities* series presents the economic wisdom of the humanities and arts. Its volumes gather the economic senses sheltered and revealed by some of the most excellent sources within philosophy, poetry, art, and story-telling. By re-rooting economics in its original domain these contributions allow economic phenomena and their meanings to come into the open more fully; indeed, they allow us to ask anew the question "What is economics?". Economic truth is thus shown to arise from the Human rather than the Market.

Readers will gain a foundational understanding of a humanities-based economics and find their economic sensibility enriched. They should turn to this series if they are interested in questions such as: What are the economic consequences of rooting economic Truth in the Human? What is the purpose of a humanities-based economics? What is the proper meaning of the "oikos", and how does it arise? What are the true meanings of wealth and poverty, gain and loss, capital and productivity? In what sense is economic reasoning with words more fundamental than reasoning with numbers? What is the dimension and measure of human dwelling in the material world?

These volumes address themselves to all those who are interested in sources and foundations for economic wisdom. Students and academics who are fundamentally dissatisfied with the state of economics and worried that its crisis undermines society will find this series of interest.

For more information about this series, please visit: www.routledge.com/Economics-and-Humanities/book-series/RSECH

A New Economic Anthropology

François Régis Mahieu

Routledge
Taylor & Francis Group

LONDON AND NEW YORK

First published 2023
by Routledge
4 Park Square, Milton Park, Abingdon, Oxon OX14 4RN

and by Routledge
605 Third Avenue, New York, NY 10158

Routledge is an imprint of the Taylor & Francis Group, an informa business

British Library Cataloguing-in-Publication Data
A catalogue record for this book is available from the British Library

ISBN: 978-1-032-47962-0 (hbk)
ISBN: 978-1-032-47963-7 (pbk)
ISBN: 978-1-003-38674-2 (ebk)

DOI: 10.4324/9781003386742

Typeset in Times New Roman
by Newgen Publishing UK

Contents

Illustrations

Figures

Tables

Note on translation

This book is a translation based on a corrected version of the work published in 2016 by L'Harmattan Editions, Paris.

This translation has benefited from the proofreading work carried out by Penelope Busby.

Introduction

From its inception in the 1940s, the anthropological approach to economics has been a place of conflicts. Anthropologists, Godelier (1974), Terray (1969), denounce the "economicism" of economists; the latter, for example, Knight (1941), rejects the multidisciplinary "descriptive" view of anthropologists.

Some economists (Nicolaï, 1999, 1974) attempted to build a bridge between the two disciplines, but they were quickly put out of action. Lévi-Strauss (2011) notes that "the debate is raging" between anthropology and economics, which he wishes were open to technical, cultural, social, and religious concerns in order to understand humankind better.

However, the nature of humankind has given rise to many theoretical discussions in political economy since the 17th century. The word anthropology[1] belongs to the vocabulary of anatomy and relates to the human body. *"It is the art that many call anthropology"* (Diderot, *Encyclopédie*, "Anatomie"). This human anatomy is characteristic of the work of William Petty, for example, in his *Political Anatomy of Ireland* (1672). Founder of political economy, he questions the scale of creatures from animals to God, including the Irish. Economic anthropology deals bluntly with the value of humankind, with the capitalized rent of activity during life! This tradition of human anatomy, specific to speculative physicians, will be abandoned by the Physiocrats in favour of the natural order and macroeconomic categories.

Rousseau (1761), whose philosophy on the natural order diverges from the conservatism of the Physiocrats, states, in the *Essai sur l'origine des langues* (1993), a rule of method constituting anthropology:

> When one wants to study men, one must look close to oneself; but in order to study man, one must learn to see far away; one must first observe the differences to discover the properties.

DOI: 10.4324/9781003386742-1

Since the "Keynesian revolution", the economy has mainly consisted of regulating the aggregates: gross domestic product, consumption, savings, foreign trade balance, debt, etc. These aggregates result from the screen accounts of the National Accounts; this functional perspective eliminates people who are covered with assumptions of generalized behaviour, for example, the use of income or the decision to invest, etc. The consequences on people are avoided. Another example: in the name of flexibility of employment, the dismissal of a worker would allow the hiring of several job seekers, but the monitoring of the new unemployed is not implemented in a country where the medicine of unemployment does not exist.

The anthropological question remains largely untreated in economics, despite the place given to the individual microeconomics, and to the person possessing capabilities (Sen, 1974) at the origin of the notion of "human" development. However, humans remain the main obstacle to economic forecasting. The anthropological approach to economics would resolve the incompleteness of economic analysis.

Our essay attempts to overcome these conflicts which have led to the virtual disappearance of economic anthropology (Hugon, 2016). It shows that these two disciplines complement each other and allow new understanding. The economy needs to go beyond the stage of *homo oeconomicus* to open to the total person.

> *You have to see what the word person means. It's what I believe to be a thinking and intelligent being, capable of reason and reflection, and who can consult himself as the same.*
> (John Locke, *An Essay Concerning Human Understanding*, 2009)

Knowledge of the person, of his/her vulnerability, of his/her suffering, of his/her possible resilience, calls on a so-called anthropological method adapted to the various sciences of human beings and society, sociology, psychology, ethnology, but not widely used in economics in a very conflictual context.[2] For example, the anthropological approach to economics shows the priority of community computing, with its constraints over the market (Meillassoux, 1975). It completes several areas neglected by economists: vulnerability, suffering, feelings, violence, etc. It complements the analysis of human behaviour by integrating psychoanalysis.

Conversely, economic theory makes it possible to enrich anthropology through its methods and models. For example, anthropology needs economics to analyse the phenomena of production and distribution in traditional societies. The question then becomes whether economic theory allows us to better understand these societies.

Thus, the work by Le Clair and Schneider (1968) shows some rare attempts at the application of microeconomics to ethnology. Nevertheless, the anthropological approach to economics goes beyond a simple observation by becoming normative through the "eminent" place given to the person, *a priori* vulnerable and suffering.

The anthropological approach to economics marks the priority of knowledge of humankind, in all its aspects, including the economic aspect, and the return to taking the subject into account. It is linked to phenomenology by privileging the human dimension of economic phenomena. It favours the subject and their feelings.

Humankind is studied as a person, an object of duty and a subject of law. Humankind is a self-aware person (the "I") and different from animals. His/her faculty of understanding is universal; it is associated with the autonomy of the will. This principle is first in anthropology, while being insufficient on its own. There exists in every individual a will that can be valued in itself. This gives him access to the moral law without it being subject to personal inclinations or to an external will. This moral law that everyone adopts, while ensuring that it is universal, translates into categorical imperatives. This recognition of universality means that, at this level, the quality of humankind comes first before any otherness relating to the society of affiliation or membership. Thus anthropology, in its recognition of universality, leads to a primary ethic: respect for humankind in his/her universal qualities. Humankind cannot be a means to an end; s/he is the end for every other person. This superiority of humankind over animals makes him/herself determine his/her own evolution by laying down rules and developing a culture. Subjecting *a priori* humankind, like an animal, to laws of evolution, subjecting his/her intellectual capacity to physical criteria (cf. the cephalic index of evolutionism), are all procedures contrary to the priorities of philosophical anthropology.[3]

There are differences according to the individuals and the societies in which they are part of; in the way of achieving "imperatives", we observe a particular behaviour of each individual in relation to standards more or less understood, accepted, assimilated. It depends on each person's personality, his/her ability to submit, his/her level of altruism and benevolence, his/her information, and his/her culture.

Based on this internalization, humankind can design a strategy for adapting standards. Thus, every individual is subject to subjective reasons which do not always coincide with objective reason; a constraint is then necessary to establish this conformity. The representation of this constraint of the will is called in Kantian terminology an "imperative". All imperatives are expressed by the verb "must" in either "categorical" or "hypothetical" form.

The hypothetical imperative is linked to a possible action as a means of achieving given ends, hypothetical or real. Economic analysis builds most of its proposals on this type of imperative: rationally combining rare means for alternative use to maximize satisfaction.

The person is multiple, like human society, its systems, structures, institutions, functions. Economic anthropology can only reduce, like other anthropologies, this complexity to a methodological fiction, most often a dualism. The best-known dualisms in anthropology take place in psychoanalysis: Freud, with the double drive of death and sex, Adler (2004) with a double personality based on the solitary thirst for power and the need for human community. Closer to economics, Bataille (1980) divides humankind between his/her ordinary useful existence and his/her pathology made of excess and violence. The phenomenological approach puts forward the hypothesis of a person immersed in the world, specifically with regard to rights and obligations. This person is fragile, vulnerable, fallible, with capacities, the loss of which reflects primarily mental suffering.

Our approach gives an importance to the suffering of the person; mainly mental suffering where psychology and psychoanalysis play a prominent role. Reducing suffering is a primary obligation. Concretely, the analysis of suffering linked to the economy, such as suffering at work or in unemployment, etc., reduces life to a series of misfortunes. People must be protected against any harm to their life. Economic life produces psychological misfortunes which substitute for the qualities of a happy life. Natural happiness, according to Philippa Foot (2014), reinforces the alienation of our contemporaries subjected to misfortune. Anthropology thus reveals a society of misfortune, contradicting the ubiquitous hedonism in economics.

The influence of the philosophical writings of Paul Ricoeur is important in our approach: his theory of constitutive capacities of the person is very general. His conception of suffering and the fragility of the person is a source of new thinking in economics; this person and his/her environment can take all the values. However, considering him/herself as fragile implies protecting him/herself, and therefore requires a normative analysis. The person makes it possible to represent the social constraints individually. S/he is both individual and structural.

The title of this work is *A New Economic Anthropology*; indeed, it is only a particular interpretation of economic anthropology, emphasizing the complementarity between the two disciplines instead of a frontal opposition and the need for a broadening of the economic problematic. This expansion concerns the subject (passage from the individual to the person), values (admission of negative values for altruism, social capital, responsibility), disciplinary references (lifting of the taboo reigning on psychoanalysis).

This expansion also concerns economic anthropology, which remains marginal compared to cultural and social approaches. Most treaties don't even mention it.[4]

The first chapter recalls the main characteristics of the person. The chosen conception of the person is inspired by phenomenology: the person is immersed in a world of rights and obligations and has the ability to assume responsibility.

Therefore, a review of the economic approach is necessary, calling into question the hedonistic principle for dealing with discontinuity and all negative values. This phenomenon is the subject of Chapter 2.

The object of our research broadens in Chapter 3 to become an anthropology of the responsible person.

Two major contributions are generally neglected in economics, vulnerability, and suffering. They complete the analysis of the person, specifically by considering the importance of psychoanalysis in the context of a person who has become responsible, vulnerable, and suffering. They will be the subject of Chapters 4 and 5.

Notes

1 In *The Nicomachean Ethics*, Aristotle creates the adjective *anthropologos* to denote pejoratively one who "speaks of humankind" by gossiping.
2 The economic debate will arise over anthropology, opposing the neoclassical approach to Marxist thought. This source of inspiration being particularly influential in France, French anthropological thought will be assimilated to Marxism; the main authors being Maurice Godelier, Emmanuel Terray, Claude Meillassoux.
3 At the beginning of the 20th century, economists, for example, Veblen, made extensive use of physical anthropology (Mahieu, 2001).
4 Florence Weber's *Brève histoire de l'anthropologie* (2015) does not mention this approach. However, there is a Society for Economic Anthropology, mainly American, which publishes the journal *Research in Economic Anthropology*.

References

Adler, A., 2004, *Connaissance de l'homme. Etude de caractérologie individuelle*, Paris: Payot, Petite bibliothèque.
Aristote, 1990, *Ethique à Nicomaque*, Paris: Librairie Philosophique Vrin.

Bataille, G., 1980, *La part maudite*, Paris: Les Éditions de Minuit.

Foot, P., 2014, *Le Bien naturel*, Genève: Labor et Fides.

Godelier, M., 1974, *Un domaine contesté: l'anthropologie économique*, Paris: Mouton.

Hugon, P., 2016, "Anthropologie et économie dans un contexte de globalisation", *L'anthropologie économique: un domaine qui reste à explorer*, Cahiers de sociologie économique et culturelle, no 59–60, Le Havre: Institut de sociologie économique et culturelle, 117–133.

Knight, F.H., 1941, "Antropology and Economics", *Journal of Political Economy*, 49: 247–268.

Le Clair, E.M., Schneider, H.K. (eds), 1968, *Economic Anthropology, Readings in Theory and Analysis*, New York: Rinehart and Winston.

Lévi-Strauss, C., 2011, *L'anthropologie face aux problèmes du monde moderne*, Paris: Editions du Seuil.

Locke, J., 2009, *Essai sur l'entendement humain*, Paris: Le Livre de Poche, Les classiques de la philosophie.

Mahieu, F.R., 2001, *Ethique économique. Fondements anthropologiques*, Paris: L'Harmattan, Bibliothèque du Développement.

Meillassoux, G., 1975, *Femmes, greniers et capitaux*, Paris: Maspero.

Nicolaï, A., 1974, "Anthropologie des économistes", *Revue Economique*, 4: 578–610.

Nicolaï, A., 1999, *Comportement économique et structures sociales (1960)*, Paris: L'Harmattan, Economie et Innovation, Série *Krisis*.

Petty, W., 1672, "Political Anatomy of Irland", in *The Petty Papers Some Unpublished Writings of Sir William Petty*. New York: A. M. Kelley, 1967.

Rousseau, J.J., 1993, *Essai sur l'origine des langues (1761)*, Paris: Flammarion, GF.

Sen, A.K., 1974, "Choice, Orderings and Morality", in Körner (ed.) *Practical Reason*, Oxford: Basil Blackwell, 54–78.

Terray, E., 1969, *Le marxisme devant les sociétés primitives*, Paris: Maspero.

Weber, F., 2015, *Brève histoire de l'anthropologie*, Paris: Flammarion, Champs: Essais.

1 Nature of economic anthropology

There is a plurality of writings favouring either subject or structure, or in other words formalism over substantivism. Anthropology is often confused with ethnology. It is closely linked to sociology as a social anthropology and its relation to economics remains marginal. This chapter returns to anthropology, as an analysis of the individual, then to economic anthropology, as the study of the person engaged in an economic activity. The ethical question relates to the nature of the person involved and his/her personal identity.

1.1 Anthropology

Anthropology, according to Kant (1798), is *"the doctrine of the knowledge of man systematically formulated"*. Kant specifies that it is about the person, capable of self-awareness. It follows that anthropology relates to the knowledge of the whole person and that it can be associated with many fields.

The person is a central concept of philosophical anthropology,[1] especially Kantian. It tends to distinguish the human species individual from other individuals, through their ability to reflect on themselves and their life with others. This is strongly reaffirmed in the first sentence of Kant's *Anthropologie du point de vue pragmatique*:

> *To possess the I in its representation: this power elevates man infinitely above all living beings on earth. By this, he is a person.*

The question of philosophical anthropology can be interpreted either as a reflection on human nature or as a reflection on the human condition. This general question is a prerequisite for a particular insight. There are endless views on the question *"What is humankind?"*, in time (primitive, modern, post-modern), in space (autonomous or heteronomous)

DOI: 10.4324/9781003386742-2

and above all, from a disciplinary point of view. It is inevitable that such a general question should be multidisciplinary and, therefore, must be examined within each scientific discipline. An anthropology can be metaphysical by asking the Augustinian question "*Who am I?*" or it can be natural or physiological by researching what nature does to humans. It poses, in its philosophical version, the question of the knowledge of humankind, "*of what man, as a being acting out of freedom, does or can and must do by himself*" (Kant, 1798). Who is this man if not a person participating in both the universality of mankind and its otherness?

Later, Claude Lévi-Strauss, in his "Introduction à l'oeuvre de Marcel Mauss" (1950), defines anthropology as:

> *An interpretation system simultaneously accounting for the physical, physiological, psychological, and sociological aspects of all behavior.*

Mauss evokes "*anthropology, that is to say the totality of sciences which consider man as a living being, conscious and unstable*". Anthropology recognizes humankind in both universality and otherness. Humankind goes beyond the stage of an anonymous individual because, as an autonomous subject, he recognizes universal norms, and as a subject capable of otherness, he internalizes and adapts the means of putting these norms into action according to his personality and his community. The universal humankind is first confronted with norms. S/he is moral, recognizing, as an autonomous being, universal norms. However, as soon as s/he participates in communities, s/he constantly faces conflicts of norms. Humankind recreates! S/he recreates his/her community, his/her society, his/her ethnicity, his/her values. These recreations are sometimes obvious: for example, the permanent recreation of ethnicity, work relationships, family. Humankind invents, in social interaction, their reaction to the most exorbitant constraints: wars, famines, pandemics.

But the recognition of humankind in his/her unity (each humankind is autonomous and capable of recognizing universal rules) implies that of his/her diversity. Every humankind is capable of internalizing rules according to his/her own characteristics and through his/her communities (of belonging and membership). This otherness accompanies universality; it poses differences and demands to be put into perspective. This inseparable couple, universality and otherness, founds anthropology and promotes mirror effects.

The explicit manifestation of customs, for example, collectivists, in any given society, allows us to understand better these implicit forms in other societies, apparently resistant to these behaviours.

1.2 The anthropological question in contemporary economic theory

If the anthropological approach to economics has been marginalized, by being assimilated to ethnology, to the study of primitive societies or even of the small peasantry, human behaviour is not absent from the contemporary economic theory; whether through the assumptions of microeconomics or the (very risky) insertion of behavioural variables in models of macroeconomics which is a bet often lost, because humankind is indifferent, s/he overreacts or resists economic policies. Economic behaviour is an inexhaustible source of criticism and an overshoot of economics, as the hypotheses it can formulate about individual behaviour, inter-individual situations, and social interactions are endless. French-speaking researchers[2] attempted to develop an economic anthropology under the leadership of André Nicolaï in the 1960s. This approach was very attached to fieldwork, rather multidisciplinary, monographic, qualitative rather than quantitative. It tried not to fall into ethnocentrism, it *"is more of an approach, a method, than a reference theory"*, according to Gastellu (1984).

Like other perspectives, economic anthropology is not a discipline; it represents a human issue from an economic perspective. Anthropology is part of an economic analysis; an unrecognized part, because the needs of the economic policy require macroeconomics. The approach is both particular from the point of view of the area of reflection and from the point of view of the method. While economic anthropology is often equated with economic ethnology, namely the study of primitive societies, it breaks away from it to deal with the person in contemporary society. According to Ricoeur (2004), the capacity for attribution increases a sense of responsibility which is a constraint on time and income; it is ahead of economists on phenomena such as vulnerability and suffering.

Ultimately, economic anthropology refocuses economics on the person and his/her life experiences. This method includes a social fact without immediately involving abstract theory and its models. Thus, *inter vivos* transfers will be included in the community system before resorting to an insurance theory; similarly, the social order based, for example, in Burundi and Rwanda, on the consumption of banana beer, must be recalled before any structural adjustment. These collective representations are the result of community pressure and not of voluntary exchange. They modify the usual explanation of the main markets, jobs, goods, services, etc. The fact of focusing on humankind, by re-situating him/her as a total person, implies lifting the taboo of psychoanalysis in economics.

Economic anthropology is positive in nature, it is based on fieldwork data but by establishing the person, it takes on a normative value. The person is universal and worthy of respect when s/he satisfies his/her rights and obligations. One of the privileged areas of the anthropological approach to economics corresponds to the theory of development, not as a comparative and relativistic analysis but as research towards otherness, of a universal economic humankind.[3] Microeconomics has an anthropological dimension when it studies humankind in his/her universality and in his/her own way of applying standards.

In fact, economic anthropology searches for universalities and the various alterations that each person brings to themselves according to his/her ethnic and linguistic origin, his/her community and the system of rights and obligations that results from it, even while confronting this approach to economic theories. The rehabilitation of humankind passes through his/her consideration as a person and no longer as an individual. How is s/he different from animals? Humankind is autonomous and expresses his/her will. In this way s/he rediscovers universal rules that s/he makes his/her own. The problem of the origin of the rules is then removed from the debate and now questions how this structure of rules is coherent.

This type of approach characterizes the first problems of the axioms of collective choices (Arrow, Sen). It finds its extension in a conception of responsibility and, more generally, in the economic theories of the person. Nevertheless, this way of thinking hardly finds its place between evolutionary perspectives and the hyper liberal current. On the other hand, many currents of economic theory develop this complexity of humankind and at the same time, his/her substantial rationality.

This complexity lies, for example, in the ability of humankind to react to signals, whether s/he is the miserable peasant in the face of lean periods or the "golden boy" of financial centres. This ability turns into expectations that destroy the surprise effect of economic policy. The power relationship of the politician and the expert over the economic agent is thwarted by the rational capacities of agents who are no longer systematically obedient objects. Consequently, economic policy no longer has the expected effectiveness on individuals supporting aggregates. This requires knowing the modes of internalization of signals and norms by humans. The economy is then phenomenological.

Another way of looking at the complexity of humankind lies in a doubling of his/her person. For example, s/he is both selfish and altruistic, constrained, and free, reasonable (enamoured of justice) and rational (in search of Good). S/he can still be a kind of travelling agent, successively visiting the family community, the labour institution, and the competitive market. The direction of the visit can be determined by rules, or better still a moral priority. Nevertheless, this priority may very well not be required: s/he can indifferently consider the doses of utility drawn from goods (his favourite food) and from people (his grandmother). S/he can still be alternately selfish and altruistic in the manner of Becker's (1974) "*spoiled-rotten child*", who fakes altruism to maximize his selfish gains. As a result, economic policy is unclear. It, for example, believes to impact the urban rich in a developing country, but forgets that the latter supports his/her rural counterparts. It opposes, in a developed economy, the retired to the unemployed, without seeing the intergenerational solidarity. Economic reflection on the human condition does not establish the passage of humankind from the state of nature to that of freedom.

The heteronomous humankind, in a natural state or in a spontaneous order, undergoes freedom; s/he did not exercise his/her free will and seek universal laws. The free humankind, expressing his/her will, does not submit to freedom and does not subject others to it, without having thought about its consequences from the point of view of the Supreme Good.

1.3 Definition of economic anthropology

Economic anthropology is defined here as a hypothetical reconstruction of the person within the framework of economic theory. In other words: economic anthropology extends the economic conception of the individual by considering the responsible person. This definition calls for many comments on the fact that the notion of the person is based on philosophical anthropology, while this consideration is limited in economics by the state of its knowledge. Put another way (and more bluntly), economic anthropology is the common subset of philosophical anthropology and the anthropology of economists.

It is out of the question to pretend to be a total and real person. If it is obvious that the person is a total fact, only aspects that may fall within the scope of method and economic theory will be considered. The economic method is hypothetical it can make assumptions on substantially economic acts (production, consumption, exchange) and more broadly, given its method, on other aspects (domestic, political, cultural, recreational, etc.) of the person. This construction can thus be very broad, but it will not show the totality, still less the reality. This person thus analysed is hypothetical (subject to prior assumptions) and cannot be real. As a result, foresight is very limited in this area and comes up against a permanent renewal of behaviour and therefore of hypotheses. But this complexity cannot be assimilated to a spontaneous "real" order. Any claim to the totality and to the dynamics of a "real" person would be extremely normative (the liberal order, for example) as it would be quickly belied by the facts. If the person is hypothetical, there are many (anthropological) clues that at the least refute the theories.

Economic anthropology needs observations, surveys, censuses, but also collections of facts about people, their abilities, and their opinions. However, here again induction (deducing collections of facts from probable laws) is a perilous exercise which cannot justify an order or an ideology. We therefore carry out here a comprehensive analysis, an "economic utopia" of the person by developing a certain number of hypotheses and method tools specific to economics. This view of the person (partial and hypothetical) diverges from any realistic conception or of claiming to be a "total person", the real complexity of which would be evident. This partial aspect aims to show the freedoms that result from the choices of the person, briefly, a personalist context of freedom, which can be envisaged with all forms of society, even the most exclusive, with the strongest constraints on political freedom or economical. This "liberal" hypothesis has no use for liberalism which imposes a liberal ideology. We can, nevertheless, make the hypothesis of a "person" who manages his/her constraints with a space of freedom. The consequences of this limited freedom (which affects the social environment) can be, for example, transfers (savings being only an uncontrolled "flight", resulting from intergenerational and intertemporal, egoism and altruism), and parallel activities or pluriactivity, most of which are informal and represent a flight out of formal production. This freedom can oppose and thwart the liberal plans of the experts. We are talking about a contemporary humankind in the name of the historical principle of recurrence: using the anthropological considerations of philosophy and economic theory, we are dealing here with a person from an economic angle.

These considerations are reinforced by mirror effects from one society to another, in particular, the alterities found in fieldwork. This conception of contemporary humankind tries to remain "neutral" from the point of view of the philosophy of history. It is out of the question to want to argue about an improvement or a deterioration of the person and of the society over time.

1.4 Economic anthropology or anthropological economics?

The question of humankind is primary in economics, both in its ancient references to *oikos* and in the contemporary principle of the optimum.

Anthropological economics tends to economize anthropology; such is the work of Gary Becker (1974) who analyses marriage, transfers, divorce, or even Barro's "theorem" on help from the old to the young (1974). An anthropological economy only integrates a human dimension to a preliminary economic question.

For example, how could a macroeconomic imbalance find a complementary understanding in the "give and take" behaviours that are initially found in markets of parallel economies? Conversely, an anthropological dimension can be reconstructed from microeconomics, by supplementing an individual's behaviour towards goods by taking others into account, by granting him the stature of a responsible person. The "dried up" concepts of individual or economic agent would thus give way to those of a humankind or a person by admitting that the utility function includes not only material arguments, but also human arguments (others).

But the recognition of humankind in his/her unity (each person is autonomous and capable of recognizing universal rules) implies that of his/her diversity. Every person can internalize these rules according to his/her own characteristics and through his/her communities (of belonging and membership). This otherness accompanies universality; it poses differences and demands to be put into perspective. This diversity is as much denied by the technocrat of an international institution who sees only the "standard" economic agent, as by the globalizing third-worldist who claims to find, for example, "Africa" or "classes". If specific interactions and communities can be posited in an ideal-typical way, such as tables distorting the facts, diversity must be posited to the individuals themselves. Economic science, for example, is too easily left with the categories of national accounts: companies, households, and State, without positing the heterogeneity and specificity of their constituent elements.

Thus, the rates of community pressure in Africa make it possible to reflect better on the individualistic American in the face of his family obligations; reciprocally, American egoism makes it possible to better understand how transfers in Africa are the result of simulated altruism (Koulibaly, 1990). There are homologies of behaviour, homologies of structure, or even of symbols, signs, and language. These homologies are one form of the quest for universality.

1.5 In search of ethics through economic anthropology

Ethics can be conceived as a search for the good life (Aristotle) or as a science of morality (Kelsen, 1996). It implies respecting each person's preference for the good life. Ethical problems can be positioned in an axiomatic framework or in an evolutionary framework: *a priori* or *a posteriori* norms?

If ethics is a priority in the social relationship, the economic calculation changes profoundly. It is a question of a lexicographical priority (Rawls, 1971), in a global perspective, or of a priority of the other in the relationship established by each person with his/her neighbour (Levinas, 1974). At this stage, the ethical requirements go beyond a simple reminder prior to the application of the economic calculation; the problem becomes that of prior ethical relationships based on responsibility towards others. These ethical reports are made of standards (obligation, prohibition, permission) which determine our elementary economic acts and make our selfish economic calculation a residual, if not utopian, element. Our acts thus relate to others (in all their subjectivity, which distances us from socio-historical totalism), to third parties (in the need for justice). Over time, our actions are situated in a network of rights and obligations, the orientation of which is anthropological, a differentiated application of universal moral laws according to the societies. The integration of ethics into the economy is thus at this price: to integrate into the most intimate concepts of economic science (utility, production, consumption, accumulation) the consequences of the intervention of the Other or more generally from the "community".

The anthropological question is also the question of the human right, as an applicant for social protection, to appreciate the economic policy offered to him. This right relates to the expression of preferences and the preservation of the equilibrium situations it obtains, taking into account, its characteristics. This right is largely compromised, either because the State unilaterally determines an objective function of social well-being, in the name of "public service", or because an international tutelage considers that it has a right of economic interference on countries in difficulty. Thus, the problem of human recognition remains unresolved in the production of information and in economic policy. This recognition is that of a full-fledged agent of the economic development of society. Humankind is "able" to express himself/herself, to react, to adapt to constraints, and this capacity is universal. The recognition of the universality of the individual is far from being settled by having an economics capable of abstract theoretical conventions. Indeed, it remains to be admitted that rationality is not reserved for an elite and is not distributed, like the first economists or Buffon's "animal economy", on a scale of decreasing dignity of creatures. The development fieldwork most clearly reveals traces of human discrimination. The "underdeveloped" is deemed "incapable" of economic rationality, whether for the technocrat overvaluing his own tools, or for the third-worldism for whom this rationality is specific to northern societies and cannot be placed on societies in the South.

Human suffering corresponds to a physical and moral degradation of the person. Medical ethics are based on the person (not the anonymous individual) and so also should economic and social ethics.

1.6 Identity

The fieldwork argument is important given the complexity of societies. Language conditions the data, ; it is the source of interpretation errors, known as "anthropological errors". In anthropology, the question of the observer's distance from his research object is the subject of numerous analyses, echoing Rousseau's thinking on this point. You must be involved in contact with the people surveyed and at the same time avoid taking yourself for one of their own. The observer remains a prisoner of his/her duties but must gain the confidence of his/her subjects. The ground is often overlooked and the quality of the data suffers. However, this quality does not consist in multiplying the explanatory factors under penalty of being subjected to the Malinvaud's paradox, which is an algorithm too loaded with explanatory factors that entails the increase in the unexplained residue. Thus, it would be preferable to use the Oxford scale to know the food needs of households rather than starting from the feeding tables according to the activities.

Anthropology helps control the "fabrication" of economic data: bad extrapolations from surveys and censuses, passive acceptance of data provided by local government. Words are essential for human action. On one hand, by creating concepts, naming objects and actions, they create an image of the world that becomes clearer through the articulation of precise concepts. On the other hand, they make it possible to exchange and communicate between people based on the articulation of these concepts, contributing to a dynamic of creation and transfers.

The two *"primary capacities"* (Ricoeur, 2004), knowing how to talk about the world, then share it based on the concepts created, do not only have positive aspects. There are errors, linked to the fallibility of the human being in expression (such as the unsaid or the double meaning) or in interpersonal understanding (misunderstandings and a double level of language). However, we cannot avoid these situations, which can be involuntary due to the fallibility of the human being (Ricoeur, 1960) and his institutions but also voluntary in a situation of domination or manipulation, when public policies are put in place. If only to achieve "institutionally sustainable" development.

Naming poses an identity problem; there is no one-to-one correspondence between names and objects: *"Part of the usefulness of language lies in its failure to copy reality into mode, one thing, one name"* (Quine, 1972). There are singular, simple, and complex terms (first level) that tend to be replaced by definitions, especially contextual (second level). Naming is done by considering the phonemes by the "system of appellations" and the "system of attitudes" (Lévi-Strauss, 1958). *"To understand the meaning of a term is always to permute it in all its contexts"* (Lévi-Strauss, 1973).

Lévi-Strauss reminds us that Marx is the first to invite us to identify symbolic systems behind language and human relationships. The commodity is thus a concept loaded with meaning, incomprehensible without its determinations (the subject of Book I of *The Capital*). A language that is rich is, therefore, capable of differentiating and individualizing, of *"discerning the indistinguishable"* (Leibniz). However, paradoxically, too much determination is detrimental; a function with too many factors of a phenomenon sees its unexplained residue increase. There is a limit where a standard analysis (cf. the Oxford scale) allows relevant results and economizes on determinations.

In this double level, we distinguish a first level of the mechanical translation of a word by a dictionary and another level where the word is placed in its context. The second level is made up of "naming effects" and "attitude effects", and these effects play out, not only in traditional societies, but also in the world of expertise where there is a competition for words within a linguistic market (Bourdieu, 1977). According to Bourdieu's comments, in this market, everyone can hold linguistic capital and expect linguistic profit from it. Speaking "properly" to the World Bank or the International Monetary Fund conditions the survival of the expert and his prospect of profit. This time it is about the sustainability of expertise!

Development begins by situating the poor in relation to the rich in the society under study. It is therefore necessary to designate people and wealth, to measure and offer activities in local languages.

There is indeed a plurality of identities in traditional societies, contrary to what Simmel (1991) argues about the assimilation of this plurality to modernity.

The dualism in terms of identity corresponds to the two axes relating to forms of identity: biographical/relational, for oneself/ for others, distributed in Figure 1.1 (formalized by the author from Dubar, 2000).

We deduce four forms of identity:

- BA: biographical for others, community type, for example, "son of";
- BS: biographical for oneself, Ricoeur's "narrative self";
- RS: relational for oneself, the reflective oneself;
- RA: relational for others, statutory identity.

In West Africa, social status is more or less differentiated; poor or rich take on a sense of community: the poor are the social orphan in this context. The children, in a context of "age groups", are all younger than I and kinship takes on a special meaning: fathers, mothers, uncles, aunts. People are designated indirectly; in the Bété legend (Paulme, 1976), the spider designates the son-in-law, the calabash, the woman. In many cases, the name of the interlocutor is not pronounced, except by the equivalent of "Thing", for example, "Ntuze" in Rundi. The name and/or first name are not only used to discern the identity of each, type BA; they can contain a story, for example, among the Baoulé of Côte

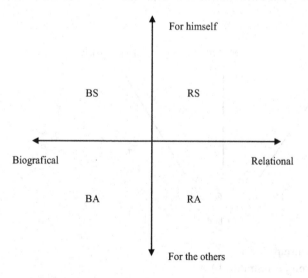

Figure 1.1 Forms of identity.

d'Ivoire, "Avouai" (pity) is given to a child whose parents have lost several children previously and who appeal to the occult powers to let him survive (Koffi, 2001). The name is often supplemented by a nickname, the "Zawlanouain", which highlights its characteristics and will be drummed by the speaker drummer (will be spoken by the speaker). Finally, the name is often the pretext to unfold a story taken up by the griot, of the BS type.

Anthropology particularly studies kinship, in particular its structure, for example, the balance of power between elders and younger children. Thus a younger poor, *a priori* can, through family solidarity, become richer than his elder. Altruism in a kinship model can be versatile without problem; thus, the child of a given couple may be rejected by the natural father and adopted by his maternal uncle or maternal grandparents, depending on the type of society or the economic situation (Figure 1.2).

A simple system of notation has been developed from the alphabetical language, intended to name exclusively relations (Table 1.1).

These eight relationships are limited to that of the nodal form of the family. Indeed, only alliance and filiation relationships are considered relevant here. Therefore, we can position any individual in his relationship with other members of the family. There is a phenomenology of measurement (time, distance, climate, etc.) that Watsuji Tetsuro (2003) reminds us of: "*The environment is thus for human beings, the moment*

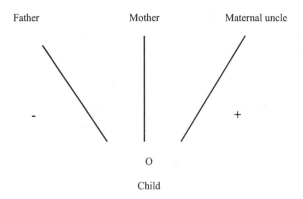

Figure 1.2 A kinship model.
Source: Based on Lévi-Strauss, 1973.

Table 1.1 Nodal form of the family

Individual		Individual	
Brother	B	Father	F
Sister	Z	Mother	M
Husband	H	Son	S
Wife	W	Daughter	D

which objects itself. This is what one should call self-discovery within the community."

For example, periods have no concrete meaning in economics. This is the case with chronological "fictions" used by theorists: day (Robertson), week (Hicks), year (Sraffa). The best-known example is John Hicks's "week" of temporary equilibrium: on the first day (Monday) prices are formed capable of equalizing the demand and supply of goods to be delivered in the week, etc. It will not be, therefore, paradoxical that the "short period" (by expected variation of returns) is longer than the "long period" (implementation of investments).

Conclusion

Like other perspectives, economic anthropology is not a discipline; it represents a human problem from an economic point of view. Economic anthropology and ethics are a part of economic analysis; a part unknown because the needs of economic policy require macroeconomics. The approach is particular, both from the point of view of the field of reflection and from the point of view of the method. Economic anthropology is not defined as an alternative to economic analysis, but as a method for broadening the field of economic theory. It gives priority to the person. This enlargement concerns the subject, with the person instead of the individual, but also the spectrum of values, by integrating the possibility of negative values, by appealing to disciplines hitherto rejected by economists and, in particular, psychoanalysis.

Economic anthropology is difficult to isolate because it is a relatively autonomous body in interaction with other anthropologies, specifically cultural and social. Take the example of the dowry in India. It is a cultural practice built on a social relationship unfavourable to women. But it is the economic constraint that drives women to abort in anticipation of the birth of a girl.

Notes

1 Bernard Groethuysen underlines in his *Philosophical Anthropology* (1953) how the injunction "know thyself" exists since reflection on oneself and human life.

2 In particular, the Office for Scientific and Technical Research in Overseas Territories, which became the French Institute for Scientific Research for Development in Cooperation and, finally, the Institute for Research for Development (IRD).

3 Development takes shape in the mind of the developer. When this "expert" realizes that he is dealing with persons capable of moral will and rationality, and not with individuals, his action takes on a universal meaning.

References

Barro, R., 1974, "Are Government Bonds Net Wealth?", *Journal of Political Economy*, 82, 6: 1095–1117.

Becker, G., 1974, "A Theory of Social Interactions", *Journal of Political Economy*, 82, 6: 1063–1093.

Bourdieu, P., 1977, "L'économie des échanges linguistiques", *Langue Française*, 34: 17–34.

Dubar, C., 2000, *La crise des identités, l'interprétation d'une mutation*, Paris: PUF.

Gastellu, J.M., 1984, "Le droit à l'économie poétique", *Approche anthropologique et recherche économique à l'ORSTOM*, Journées d'étude, 13 et 14 décembre 1984, Collection Colloques et Séminaires, éditions de l'ORSTOM.

Groethuysen, B., 1953, *Anthropologie philosophique*, Paris: Gallimard-Tel.

Kant, E., 1993, *Anthropologie du point de vue pragmatique (1798)*, Paris: GF-Flammarion.

Kelsen, H., 1996, *Théorie générale des normes*, Paris: PUF, Léviathan.

Koffi, B.A., 2001, *L'univers des noms et prénoms Baoulé en Côte d'Ivoire*, Abidjan: NEI.

Koulibaly, M., 1990, *Le libéralisme, nouveau départ pour l'Afrique noire*, Paris: L'Harmattan, Afrique 2000.

Levinas, E., 1974, *Autrement qu'être, ou au-delà de l'essence*, La Haye: Nijhoff.

Lévi-Strauss, C., 1950, "Introduction à l'œuvre de Marcel Mauss", in M. Mauss (ed.), *Sociologie et anthropologie*, Paris: PUF, ix–lii.

Lévi-Strauss, C., 1958, *Anthropologie structurale*, Paris: Plon.

Lévi-Strauss, C., 1973, *Anthropologie structurale, II*, Paris: Plon.

Paulme, D., 1976, *La mère dévorante, essai sur la morphologie des contes africains*, Paris: Gallimard-Tel.

Quine, W.V.O., 1972, *Méthodes de logique*, Paris: Armand Colin, Coll. U.

Rawls, J., 1971, *A Theory of Justice*, Belknap Press, Harvard University.

Ricoeur, P., 1960, *Philosophie de la volonté 2, Finitude et culpabilité, l'homme faillible*, Paris: Aubier.

Ricoeur, P., 2004, *Parcours de la reconnaissance*, Paris: Stock.

Simmel, G., 1991, *Secret et sociétés secrètes*, Strasbourg: Circé.

Watsuji, T., 2003, "La signification de l'éthique en tant qu'étude de l'être humain", *Philosophie*, Paris: Editions de Minuit, 79: 5–24.

2 Anthropology and economic theory, a difficult association

Economic anthropology is a minor part of the anthropological literature; this can be understood in the context of a primitive society where
the economy does not appear distinctly. However, the reason for this
minorization is that economic theory has its dogmas, notably utilitarianism and hedonism, which opposes the anthropological approach.
Economics has lost a human point of view for a functional method.
A broadening of the economic calculation is necessary. We cannot stay
with the ideal of continuity, given the priorities set out in the calculation
over the others. Discontinuity characterizes the whole of consumption,
but also the world of work. Ricoeur becomes an economist by insisting
on the link between personal choice and collective decisions, a link
which should favour prospective rather than planning. Given the conflict mentioned above, it is difficult to combine economics and anthropology. How far can we integrate anthropology into economics without
questioning the foundations of economic reasoning?

2.1 The difficulties of an association between economics and anthropology

While economics is hypothetical and claims to issue general laws,
applicable to all societies, anthropology applies a principle of reality
and relativizes laws.

2.1.1 Is economics a-anthropological?

Economics is concerned with a rational agent, made up of understanding.
It is interested in the autonomous agent, the one who accesses, beyond
the senses, categorical imperatives.

Anthropology studies the deformation by humankind in a
(heteronomous) society of universal rules; deformation linked to

DOI: 10.4324/9781003386742-3

hypothetical imperatives, to the means of satisfying its (universal) ends, to its perversities.

It is easy to identify the parts of economic theory where men are absent as direct actors. The a-anthropological plus is the system of Sraffa (1970) which deals with the production of commodities by commodities. In a system of this type, only technical relationships established on the basis of a standard measurement are involved.

More generally, macroeconomics moves away from anthropology because it is based on global variables and aggregates, not on people. This is the goal of national accounting by playing on screen accounts and balances which do not show the men themselves, but institutional sectors.

The categories, companies, households, public administrations, are heterogeneous, and the fact of attributing to them generalized behaviour assumptions poses serious problems. These assumptions are inherent in the Keynesian theory, the main inspiration for this method. Thus, the fundamental relationships relate to aggregate quantities, for example, the equivalences between aggregate income and either the sum of consumption and investment, or the sum of consumption and savings. The risk of error is all the greater as the forecast is based on past accounts and likely trends in the economy; the behavioural variable is difficult to predict with such categories.

Fundamental psychological laws, including the superiority of the propensity to save over the propensity to consume, or fundraising behaviours, are the subject of controversy.

In this macroeconomic framework, the interactions and therefore the reactions of individuals to their constraints are not taken into account. In this retroactive set, the problems of redistribution are complex and the totality of the analytical instruments will not reveal them. A good example of this conceptual difference is the treatment of savings in Keynesian macroeconomics as a fatal balance between aggregate income and aggregate consumption. On the contrary, an "individual" conception of savings can make this "sacrifice" appear as arising from precaution, from insurance, from a guarantee to be taken in a trade-off between intertemporal and intergenerational disturbances. Both global stimulus policies (in developed countries) and adjustment or stabilization policies (in developing countries) have very limited economic efficiency and questionable social effects. Their effectiveness is limited by the capacity of agents to react to constraints and to anticipate policies, in the name of their individual interest and other broader considerations (responsibility) to their personality. They are mostly blind and cannot take into account the interests of people. However, people are present at the level of policy issuance, expressing conflicts of interest, simulated altruisms; nothing to do with the level of individuals subject to such policies. Macroeconomics considers that it does *a priori* for the good of individuals. It decrees their well-being and sets itself up as a public service for the masses.

2.1.2 Humankind, the troublemaker

The idea of the secret garden, or of the strategic reactions of economic agents, does not appear until very late. If the individual (the economic agent) establishes his/her economic mores (consumption, production, savings, transfers) according to his/her environment, inevitably moral standards come into play. The result is a network of moral constraints in addition to purely material ones. These moral constraints, depending on human behavior, can become material (donations, transfers). However, these externalities are rarely considered in economic theory; the calculation on moral constraints is complex, it depends on information, handling, socio-family status, etc.

Economic ethics studies the customs (ethos) of humankind under the constraints of nature and the community of human beings. It therefore seeks both an economic human universality (for example in the gift or the market) and an alterity in human behaviour, at given times and in given places. It studies economic behaviour by favouring the economic role (maximization under constraints broadened to socio-ethics), but cannot replace a general anthropology, based on totality and history. However, the economy is too often standard and differential. Standard is not universal; it lacks the standards that underpin the universality of gender human, otherwise the standard applies only to hypothetical imperatives and therefore to otherness.

The "I", thanks to reason, establishes otherness and the fundamental difference between humankind and all things. Humankind is in economics, an indistinct part of global entities (basic economic units: households, companies, institutions) and sometimes an individual in social interaction (Becker, 1974), but that economics forces us to recognize him/her as "out of the norms". Without doubt, if s/he is manipulated by the "invisible hand" or unconsciously produced structures, s/he is only *homo oeconomicus*. S/he is determined mechanically by the market or the mode of production.

But humankind is a troublemaker. S/he resists economic policy and even more invalidates it through his/her capacity for learning, his/her anticipations and his/her overreactions. After the intellectual modes of structuralism and analytical introspection, economism could be triumphant if it were not for the hazards posed by humankind in both civil society and the society of needs. The failure of structuralist models, and more generally of macroeconomic policies, is largely rooted in humankind; the latter is present just as much in the providers of economic policy as in the applicants. Humankind is present with his/her natural selfishness and constantly twists the best ideas to his/her benefit. S/he is also present as a social being, a constitutive element of societies that develop their particularisms and their resistances. While macroeconomics can hardly take humankind into account, it is not certain that microeconomics is automatically anthropological. One can easily imagine the risk of a universality transformed into standardization, of paying attention only to rules (maximization under constraints) or universal norms (optimum) out of all otherness and meaning of ground.

2.1.3 Is microeconomics an economic anthropology?

Microeconomics seeks a standard view of individual or household behaviour but it does not take into account the strategic behaviour of the agent until very late. The interest of this massive integration, notably through game theory, is to show the irreducibility of behaviour to laws, the difficulty in finding unique solutions. The analysis of the interaction of individual behaviours quickly becomes inextricable as soon as one leaves the ultra-simplified framework of the usual presentations in game theory.

If economic anthropology is the study of humankind from an economic perspective, it merges with economic theory when the latter is based on humankind. The fact of studying economic acts by emphasizing an ideal-typical point of view is a principle of economics. Anthropology, through its ambitious object (humankind), represents an immense field that the researcher can only modestly consider, even if he is aware of the interconnection of the fields studied. Totalism cannot be, except through mastery of state and movement, a program of study. Likewise, the social sciences cannot, according to Weber, establish an ultimate cause in the chain of causalities (Weber, 1992).

Thus, anthropology and ethics are pragmatic, unless one embraces humankind in his/her totality, human society in its infinity and all its complexity. A point of view is inevitably privileged. There is therefore an anthropology from the economic point of view; pragmatically, this is carried out by the economists themselves in their community, with their instruments.

Microeconomics fits naturally into an anthropological framework by studying economics at the level of individuals, their preferences, their individual acts, their interactions (market, plan, vote, transfers, informal strategies). On the condition that it is both a universal instrument (for example by considering situations "as if") and an understanding of otherness, microeconomics, in the field of economics, makes it possible to understand through ideal-types is a philosophical concept.

Microeconomics concerns the individuals themselves or the forms of their interactions (contract, market, plan) or even the places of these (households, businesses, communities, etc.); it has an understanding nature. In comparison, macroeconomics is closer to economic policy and therefore to normative concerns; it provides the rationale for the Leviathan.

This positivity of microeconomics makes it a critical instrument of macroeconomics. The market, the optimum, and well-being can be formidable critical instruments, the bad conscience of the macroeconomist, but microeconomics has often been frowned upon; its users consider it only as a method, applicable to the search for a planned as well as a market equilibrium. However, it presupposes a philosophy of life (the search for happiness) or a conception of society; Arrow and Sen, for example, are on the borderline of economics and philosophy. The formalization of microeconomics is necessary, as are its extreme assumptions. Formalizing abstraction makes it possible to synthesize situations and to identify possible variations in relation to extreme assumptions. For example, pure and perfect competition makes it possible to understand the imperfections of competition. Typifying a corner optimum situation (e.g. poverty optimum) allows us to better situate the paradoxes of poverty. The individual optimum and the compensation for any externality constitute the finality of all economic reasoning. Microeconomics considers any action or situation from the point of view of its consequences for the optimum of the group considered. Economic anthropology deals not only with behaviour and actions, but systematizes preferences, resentments, envy, or even frustration.

It is not enough for microeconomics to consider elementary units of economic analysis. These units must be human (and not just individual) and fulfil the qualities of philosophical anthropology (universality and otherness). Most often, it only retains the standard aspect, a universality, without enriching itself in the understanding of otherness; but also, betraying Hume's rule, his understanding (positivity) becomes normative. Microeconomic entities can be formed without men: companies abstracted from all behaviour, organizations, institutions and very quickly these categories belong to macroeconomics by their hypotheses of generalized behaviour. Economic anthropology would be poor if it were reduced to individual economic calculation, for example, the equalization of the weighted marginal utilities of the consumer against possible goods, or the conditions of his optimal personal equilibrium. This case of "robinsonnade" is exceptional. The Other intervenes very quickly, either to analyse Robinson's intrapersonal comparisons, or, more naturally, to share time, goods, etc. with Robinson. From then on, the microeconomics broadens considerably to become a public economy focusing on the modalities of sharing. Too often critics of the "microeconomic robinsonnade" are unaware that the essence of microeconomics lies in its social component: the gigantic nebula of public economy and social economy.

Microeconomics deals with a complex "personality". Most often, this person is a dualist, made up of social constraints and free choices. This moral economy which characterizes the economy is "contra-dictory", made up of constraints and strategies of free choice. The "person" for Roemer is composed of a "social type" and a freedom that comes at its cost: responsibility. The same is true for the Becker's consumer who, faced with his social environment, "produces" utilities. The economic personality is therefore complex in this dual mode; the question being how to model this duality. From a technical point of view, we have to imagine a second-order calculation (ordinality or coordinality[1]) and a questioning of the possibilities of switching from the axiomatic of preferences to marginal calculus (continuity or lex-icographic priority?).

Opening up the microeconomics means integrating into it the constraints of other areas, for example, political, demographic, sexual. These constraints occur on a preference function whose arguments can be choices of society, of principles, of people. Once again, the individu-alist angle is only intended to better enrich social constraint, to better understand its internalization.

2.1.4 A difficult expansion of economic calculation

The person makes choices that s/he hopes to find in collective decisions. This requirement is the basis, according to Ricoeur, of foresight. "*Forecasting multiplies choice*" and promotes the link between personal choices and collective decisions. Ricoeur celebrates "*the increased cap-acity for choice*" determined by a social morality; it is about an ethic of responsibility and a fight against dehumanization. Two dogmas are questionable from the point of view of economic anthropology: con-tinuity and the rejection of negativity.

The assumption of continuity is *ad hoc* for marginalism, that is to say, for the individual calculation, but is terribly restrictive regarding the relation of choice as posited by Arrow. This expresses a relation of choice between a variable number of individuals and an infinity of situations. The dogma of continuity considerably restricts the expression of choices in economics. This continuity is close; it forces far-fetched hypotheses, for example, the non-survival of the consumer, who has the free choice between surviving or not surviving. This continuity makes it possible to substitute doses of goods in the choice between goods. However, this is no longer valid as soon as the choice is presupposed on people. These calculations involve priorities. In fact, it is about recognizing the discontinuity, whether in the realm of consumption or of work. Work is more and more marked by interruptions and changes in profession, place of residence, etc.

Discontinuity becomes the rule and continuity the exception.

The same problem arises with the spectrum of values. The economic calculation waited a century to integrate altruism, between Marshall (1890) and Becker (1974), Barro (1974) and Buchanan (1975). This integration takes place at two levels: that of the dogma of an inevitably positive altruism and that of a continuity formed from characteristics. Negative altruism admits malice, perversion, or even sadism. Likewise, social capital, utility, or even responsibility can take on values across the spectrum of values: whether they be positive, neutral, or negative. This negativity is strongly condemned by Harsanyi in his later writings (1995), in the name of hedonism.

2.2   How can anthropology be better associated with economics?

The association of anthropology with economics is thwarted either by an anti-economist ethnology or by a globalizing economy. The first explicit (Veblen, 1899) or implicit (Austrian praxeology) attempts in this direction failed.

2.2.1   *A difficult association*

What are the main differences between the individual in economic theory and the person in economic anthropology? This person is based on responsibility in a society of rights and obligations. S/he has, according to Ricoeur, a fragile structure of capacities. As a result, the individual is vulnerable and potentially suffering; s/he must be protected by the application of a precautionary principle and the recognition of economic crime. The useful "everything" must be secondary to the reduction of suffering.

The status of the actors determines the economic calculation; for example, treating them as selfish and opportunistic individuals or as responsible and constrained people changes the type of economy. Changes occur at all levels: value, distribution, main functions relating to work, goods and services, finance, etc. Economists have assumed the radical idea of the de-alienation of the individual, rejecting to the rank of moral economics when involving religious or moral determinations. This status of a completely secularized individual is only a radical assumption, taken from the "Age of Enlightenment". It allows a simplified economic calculation, but neglects community solidarity.

If one considers a responsible person instead of the opportunistic individual, utility is no longer the only primary factor of an exogenous nature. Usefulness depends on a person's rights (R) and obligations (O), and therefore on the responsibility that will be attributed to him/her. The calculation of his/her rights and obligations depends on societal or local standards which show community pressure. This pressure can be likened to a voluntary exchange if taking on his/her R/O expresses his/her freedom. The utility is therefore endogenized and results from his/her calculation of R/O. The person is not only responsible, but also rational and reasonable, and is situated at a level which cannot return to the society of nature, nor to sociobiology. Solidarity nourishes responsibility, economic individualism destroys it.

In general, economic theory addresses only one side of anthropology:

- Either it only privileges the autonomy of the humankind and his/her capacity to reach a universal rationality, by refusing the "polylogism" (Von Mises, 1949) or by systematically seeking standard behaviours, such as the research of the World Bank type of Living Standard Measurement Studies across all developing economies.
- Or it only examines pure otherness, cultural differences, in the manner of intercultural management, of ethnography assimilated to anthropology, and especially of Veblen's evolutionary anthropology.[2]

Economic anthropology, according to Godelier (1974), contests the universality of the concepts of economic theory and is interested only in otherness, assimilated to the marxian sociohistorical relativization. Opposed to economist universalism is an equally universalist fundamentalism (the deep and hidden structures of the capitalist mode of production); these same structures enable the rereading of all the others.

Institutionalist theory and Austrian theory were two missed opportunities in economic anthropology, due to excess of alterity and universality, respectively. It is not enough to invoke the complexity of the person to make him/her a "black box" or a pretext for absolute liberalism; it is not enough either to assert the universality and alterity of humankind. We must draw the consequences in the understanding of economic acts. The autonomous economic agent always retains a margin of freedom in his actions and must reconcile this freedom with his network of rights and obligations; the person is made of freedom and responsibility in his/her relationship to others.

Philosophical anthropology is an uncommon consideration in economic theory. Economic anthropology has been appropriated most often by ethnologists, with reference to distant ethnic groups or the evolution of European races (Vacher de Lapouge, 1897), in order to denounce economic theory. Conversely, the approach to economic problems in crisis contexts has been largely aggregative and planning. The "macroeconomic closure" does not matter anthropologically. Anthropology as the study of "man" seemed far removed from a standard microeconomics based on disembodied "agents" or "individuals", calculating their individual equilibrium in isolation before meeting in one market and then in all markets. This caricatured reference to *homo oeconomicus* ignores the many in-depth microeconomics known as "public economy", dealing with the individual (Arrow, Sen), social interaction (Becker, Barro), and the person (Rawls, Roemer). A major economic school simultaneously developed the critique of macroeconomic "planning" and denounced the reduction of the complexity of humankind to an individual mechanism, notably the contemporary Austrian school with Von Mises and Hayek. The latter explicitly refers to cultural anthropology.

More generally, the economic theory of modern society, in particular of industrial competition, has been largely influenced by sociobiological theories, in particular Herbert Spencer (1891). Already Marshall (1890) made extensive use of the themes of the struggle for life, themes taken up in contemporary sociobiology of altruism as fitness. Previously, Marshall closed the debate on the necessary integration of altruism and moral values (preface to the first edition of the *Principles*) by definitively affirming the principle of continuity in economics. No priority (or lexicographical order) relating to moral reasons can be established in the economic calculation; there is no break between behaviours, classes, normal or abnormal, between normal or occasional values. The axiom of continuity of microeconomic calculus has the immense practical advantage of allowing the passage between an axiom of preferences and a differential analysis of utilities.

The taking into account of the "nature" of humankind is carried out in economic theory, by integrating some assumptions of morality (hedonism, utilitarianism, benevolence) and rationality. However, the debate only becomes interesting on the type of socialization: interindividuality, interaction, cooperation. Therefore, the corresponding places (household, business, city, market, government) are more objects of analysis than man himself. It is then a question of "social household" (Myrdal, 1953), of "catallaxy" (Von Mises and Hayek), of the intergenerational, in short, of a theory of the human condition (Arendt, 1958), or of the human action (Von Mises, 1949).

2.2.2 Economic anthropology and economic theory: the conditioned humankind of social interaction

According to H. Arendt (1958), Saint Augustin is the first to pose the anthropological question in philosophy, distinguishing two questions about humankind, "*Who am I?*" and "*What am I?*". Questioning human nature consists of freeing our nature from all the objects that surround us. This anthropological question, "*Who am I?*" arises, according to Arendt, in front of God. If a part of myself escapes me, I can only put it down to the presence of God. This question therefore escapes economic anthropology and is more a matter of metaphysics. The question "*What am I?*" relates to the human condition; of humankind in his/her "social household" (Myrdal), and more generally of his/her activities. If Arendt distinguishes between labour, work, and action in the *vita activa*, Von Mises, in a radically different way, places actions in "catallaxy". The condition of humankind or of the "social household" leads to an apparent paradox: the more determined person is, the more important it becomes to go through his/her mode of internalization in order to illuminate and understand the individual game. Individualism is therefore only a method for better understanding the capacities of humankind in the face of his/her multiple social constraints. This power over constraints and this ability to accommodate determinisms most often escapes technology. To better understand the behaviour of men, statistical data can now be entered, checked, cleared, processed, and analysed with high-performance computer processes. Instead of several years, a few hours are enough in the realization of these operations.

But the anthropological basis of these surveys is still weak. The most elementary anthropological effects make the questions irrelevant and the answers unsuitable: effects of naming, memory, equivocity of the units of time and place. The questionnaires are all the more vague as their processing is powerful. Being put into cards and ready-made formulas is all the stronger and humankind is lucky if s/he can escape. Thus, according to Malinvaud (1991), *"The observation of decision-making methods reveals that the difficulty of relevant information is more important than the difficulty of this calculation"*.

Economic anthropology can be situated in the privileged historical places of human economic expression: the household, the underdeveloped society.

What is the economic practice of the household? Gunnar Myrdal (1953) asks the question:

> *What does a social economy whose function is the social household mean? First, it implies or suggests an analogy between the individual who manages his property or that of his family and his company. Adam Smith and J.S. Mill made this analogy explicitly.*

However, this conception has often been undermined by philosophies of history. The individual would be invaded by modernity and his home, *oikos*, exposed to the public face. Thus, many post-war works developed Baudrillard's idea of humankind crushed by the production society, of work by work, if not "obscene"; such as TVs or talk shows where everyone comes to show off their privacy. To this prophecy of modernity, assimilated to the socialization of the private, answers the idea of the *"private, more and more private"* (Simmel, 1991) or the idea that the private has always been private (Hayek, 1960, in reference to Sapir on the universality of property).

Public or secret, the household is not the only place of social interaction that may be of interest to economic anthropology. The importance of intergenerational calculations in a crisis leads us to return to extended families, and to evoke dynasties. There are functional places of interaction (companies, administrations, sports clubs, etc.) and decision-making methods (market, vote, plan). It is with these places like societies, that they can be considered globally by their aggregated results and/or as so many knots of contracts and conflicts that enable knowledge of the human condition. Thus, gift/counter-gift strategies in the entrepreneurial relationship or in politics (logrolling for example) make it possible to better understand the human condition. Mirror effects or complementarities can be sought. So, when economists (Becker) are interested in "the spoiled child", they have every interest in enriching their hypotheses (while keeping their method) on other anthropological points of view, the search for fame, thirst for power, etc., to understand better the nature of the couple egoism/altruism.

Anthropology's ground of excellence is all the more "primitive society" as knowledge of humankind is assimilated to ethnology. Without taking into account the difficult relationship between the tendencies of ethnology and economic analysis, economics since the postwar period has not considered the primitive economy, but "developing economies".

Indeed, during this period, the "*lower caste*" (Bardhan, 1993) of development economists provided economists with many anthropological tools, such as the gift/counter-gift in labour economics causing a fundamental change in the analysis of unemployment. Reciprocally, development economics no longer constitutes the anthropological "exception" to economic rationality, the latter being able to be conceived as a simple adaptation to constraints or as hyper rationality (e.g. rational anticipation by lean season planters). It is no longer conceivable to consider that the "underdeveloped", like the "class itself" of the proletarians, are below rationality or the "threshold of consciousness", and that it is up to an avant-garde of experts or politicians to bring them awareness. As a result, knowledge of humankind from an economic point of view is carried out in all societies without the level of development being in question. The assumption of minimal (universal) rationality is not enough, people considered in this way have an economic dimension which leads them to cooperate in their society, with a view to their mutual benefit.

2.2.3 Economic anthropology in the face of conflicts of method

The anthropological question cannot be enclosed in methodological conflicts such as inductivism/deductivism, holism/individualism, or even comparative realism/hypothetical method. Nor does it belong to a particular discipline (medicine, psychology, sociology or ethnology). In economics, the anthropological question (*What is humankind?*) is treated hypothetically by many theories, mainly microeconomic. The same is true for economic ethics, which questions the possibility of a moral economy. This issue remains very much in the minority and is opposed to a-anthropological economic theories (material, aggregative, holistic, systemic, etc.).

We will therefore deal with the historical opposition between anthropology and economics, with the contemporary terms of this opposition, and finally with what economic anthropology is pragmatically, within the economic theories of the interindividual and of social interaction.

The anthropological point of view in economics deals with the mores of economic humankind in his/her universality and his/her otherness. This associative character of anthropology leads to the dissolution of a certain number of conflicts of method, constitutive of the social sciences: holism versus individualism, historical evolution versus ethnocentric recurrence.

Take the old conflict between holism and individualism. The anthropological point of view postulates the individual and his autonomy (in universality) in his capacity to create the social (even unconsciously) and to adapt its constraints. Humankind is the obligatory crossing point for standards, even if they are the expression of very strong social constraints. Anthropology studies how humankind internalizes norms, allowing the individual to analyse social norms through his/her societal network. Anthropology does not oppose the individual to the social; methodological individualism consists of using the individual as a representation of social constraints.

Universality does not constitute an ethnocentric point of view, but the inevitability which presides over a recurrent reading based on the progress of reason. Ethnocentrism can creep into internalizations and deviations; for example, one can estimate that family relations are of the same nature in Africa and North America. The mirror effect plays in space, but also in time. History teaches us that there are universals in past economic behaviour and specific modalities in their adaptation. The specific modalities of exchange (potlatch, kula), destruction (bilabia), the facilities of certain areas of abundance (Sahlins, 1972) allow us to understand better the adaptation of the general principles of maximization under constraint. The gift, conspicuous consumption, the destruction of the surplus, have political and cultural purposes that we must understand.

Anthropology thus studies humankind in his/her universality and his/her otherness; economic, it relates these characteristics to economic pragmatics, everyday economic acts. These acts are therefore normative; the task of economic tools, from this perspective, therefore consists of emphasizing universality and otherness.

2.2.3.1 What is humankind? Status of methodological individualism

The question of the economic humankind is inevitable. The scarecrow of *homo oeconomicus* has relegated it to the radius of dangerous abstractions. However, this question is primary. Humankind is capable of thinking and the expression of his/her preferences in economic theory appeals to his/her totality. How can we denounce both the economic reductivism of *homo oeconomicus* and the broader application of economics to all areas of social life?

In the social sciences, it is common to oppose the social to the individual, nominalism to social realism. The problem easily becomes a debate on the genesis of the social, atomism versus molecular, or the reduction of the whole to the elements (cf. the debate around the *Gelstat Theory*). This debate on the method of apprehending the social was systematized by Maurice Godelier in *Rationality and irrationality in economics* (1965) by opposing *homo oeconomicus* to the socio-historical totality as a starting point for the analysis of society. In economics, this debate is fundamentally about the lack of a bridge between micro and macroeconomics, between the problem of general equilibrium (Walras) and that of global equilibrium (Keynes). A debate on the microeconomic foundations of macroeconomics was introduced from the mid-1960s (Clower, 1970), on the ability to make Keynes a special case of Walras. This debate between micro and macroeconomics, or between structure and individual, is overtaken by the anthropological dimension. In this context, it is not a question of contesting the existence of the Other or even the social norms which follow, but to refine the analysis by carefully examining how each, according to the Other, internalizes the social, the rights, and obligations that result from it.

It is therefore necessary to understand how each humankind represents the social in a form which is proper to him/her, specific, while being treated by a universal method. This is the method of representing norms that is suggested by showing cases of strictly individual configuration (no one can have the same time allocation scheme, the same social network, etc.).

2.2.3.2 Microeconomic foundations of macroeconomic imbalances

In the field of economic understanding, economic anthropology is a particular point of view which cannot replace that, for example, of macroeconomics, particularly in the field of development.

Anthropology makes it possible to relativize the universal point of view by taking into account othernesses. Economic anthropology internalizes macroeconomic constraints at the level of people and externalizes individual deformations at the level of a meso or macroeconomic entity, market, community, sector, branch, or aggregate. Nevertheless, this interrelation was evacuated based on a postulate of a lack of a bridge between the two fields, of a-anthropological macroeconomics or even of standard microeconomics. Macroeconomic imbalances are most often posed "by helicopter", for example, with the hypothesis of a markup of companies. Yet they are found in interpersonal relationships themselves, relationships avoided in the name of a so-called black box.

The human condition is at the centre of economic analysis, a question that macroeconomics avoids. In fact, behind the aggregates, it is possible to enter the "black box" of people and interpersonal relationships; this rise in the chain of causes leads to making assumptions about personal constraints and original imbalances. Institutions, organizations, communities, and other social forms are relevant units of observation of economic agents and their interactions. Thus, the household, the company, the government are not only "screen" units, the performance of which can be observed without questioning how they are obtained. They are places of contract or conflict, of struggle or cooperation. The circumstances and economic processes within these institutions form the subject of an economic anthropology particularly suited to the tools of microeconomics: marginal analysis, axioms of choices, strategic theories.

An economic anthropology that claims to reject the tools of microeconomics would deny itself the possibility of studying the main economic problems relating to humankind, especially his/her choices under constraint, in the context of his/her personality.

Conversely, when microeconomics refuses the person and reduces him/her to a standard individual, it avoids the anthropological question.

On anthropological bases (Mauss, 1950; Geertz, 1996), many areas of economic reflection have been turned upside down by the consideration of interpersonal relationships. Thus, labour relations in companies have been analysed, since Akerlof (1984), behind an informal contract such as implicit gift/counter-gift bargaining. Likewise, behind governments, economic analyses have highlighted similar behaviours of logrolling, rent-seeking, corruption, patronage, and paternalism of all kinds. The most recent example is that of households and the interindividual strategies carried out by their members in the face of economic constraints, in particular playing on the "tender" cards (transfers) and the "time" card (activities).

In all cases, inter-living transfers (20% of GDP in the United States, more than 100% of income for some officials in the Third World) disturb economic agents. Their social environment obliges them to constrain their most basic economic acts: production, consumption, savings, investment, etc. They must therefore arbitrate between the "selfish" disturbances caused by the temporal postponement of their enjoyments and the "altruistic" disturbances caused to the obligees by their immediate enjoyment and find an individual equilibrium savings rate. This type of calculation depends on the strength of sociability relationships and affective elements that are difficult to quantify.

These elements create an individual sociability map for everyone, consisting of reciprocal obligations and on which a strategic choice is made. Income and time constraints make it necessary to choose, hide, or exaggerate. Any attack on individual balance by economic policy or other exogenous events are immediately integrated by the individuals who react. The meaning of this reaction can be, for example, a preservation "step by step" of the transfers made to certain people of the sociability map. The quantification and understanding of these transfers, most of which are "informal", remains a major problem. On average 10% to 20% of the use of income escapes the political will!

The "tender" card is not the only strategic possibility; the personality is exercised in a choice over time. The many discoveries on informal production (in most cases, a pluriactivity) aggravate the difficulties of economic policy. This time, production-consumption, a market and income escape statistical recording. This reaction takes place on the individual time map. The margin of freedom that exists on the individual time card is important in certain situations, especially in rural areas, and informal economies represent an important part of the national economy. The time card is particularly flexible in an informal setting and allows a remarkable reaction to any constraint, and in particular to economic policy. To what extent will the reduction in working time, for example, in the construction industry, translate into an increase in informal work? Conversely, considering that every person's schedule is saturated, it is difficult to know what his reaction will be to additional strain on his time allocation.

Transfers and pluriactivity intersect and can complement each other. Faced with his economic constraints, every individual has this leeway, to use his entourage and/or to use the time at his disposal. If the state grants large subsidies to citizens, the use of other strategies (formal income, informal transfers, pluriactivity) will become less urgent. Thus, the relationship between informal strategies (transfers, pluriactivity) and formal strategies (formal individual income, state transfers) delimits the endowment (the possibilities) that a person uses in the face of his/her constraints. Considering that this endowment corresponds to a given subsistence minimum, any decrease in one of its components (state subsidy for example) results, unless it disappears, in an increase in other income possibilities (private transfers, individual income, informal pluriactivity). However, the form of this recomposition cannot be predicted mechanically in the name of the relative freedom of people. The building is all the more fragile as the situation is miserable.

2.3 The method: from conflicts to complementarity

Is there an incompatibility between the methods of anthropology and those of economics?

Anthropology favours the principle of reality; economics is hypothetical. To the abstraction of economists, we oppose the concrete search for differences. Anthropology is primarily a study of humankind. This person is not necessarily social, contrary to what Lévi-Strauss asserts (example: the responsibility of the person in relation to himself/herself in Sartre). Anthropology studies him/her in his/her unity and diversity. It respects him/her in his/her dignity as a person, in his/her authenticity, outside any ethnocentrism. It is based on the direct observation of social behaviour from a human relationship and, as a study of the person, promotes economic tools.

2.3.1 Anthropology favours personal experience in the field

It favours comprehensive surveys (for example by monitoring a panel) rather than representative. The field involves blending in with the social group being studied in order to ensure the objectivity of the analysis. "*Anthropology seeks to develop the social science of the observed*" (Lévi-Strauss, 1958).

It prefers to work with people on a daily basis, in the name of local rationality. These people are entitled to respect in the name of an ethics of statistics (Tolstoï, 1892; Goulet, 1965). It refers to the totality, to the "total social fact", but does not claim to capture it. The totality does not mean "*totalism*" but a totality constructed by interactions between structures and behaviours. Anthropology is about "*all men*" and "*all man*" as Lebret (1968) puts it.

It conducts comparative analyses, much like Kluckhohn's (1985) mirrored anthropology: I understand my society better by understanding others.

Lévi-Strauss, in his project to teach anthropology, recalls the qualities to be observed:

- Objectivity: it is necessary to rise above methods of thought and abstract notions, especially in economics, for example, marginal productivity. The anthropologist seeks meaning from a semiological perspective.
- Totality: instead of breaking it up into pieces as economists do, it is necessary "to discover a form common to the various

manifestations of social life"; here we find the total social fact initiated by Marcel Mauss.

- Meaning: societies are founded on personal relationships, particularly in the case of so-called primitive societies.
- Authenticity: it is necessary to work on relevant social groups and not to abuse studies of a national character; what Geza Roheim denounces (1978) about the work of Margaret Mead on Americans, or Ruth Benedict on Japan.

Other principles can be formulated:

- Reciprocity: the observation relates to the observed and the observer.
- Reflexivity: takes into account the characteristics of the observer.
- Relative autonomy of anthropology vis-à-vis sociology.
- Universality: possible applications to all societies.

2.3.2 Complementarity of methods in the understanding of the person

To understand a person in a social interaction, economic anthropology is only one method (Gastellu, 1984). Lévi-Strauss (1958) insists on the rapprochement of anthropology with the new formulation of economic problems, notably game theory.

The identity of each person begins with his/her kinship relationships; it appears in an interplay of rights and obligations between generations.

Thus the responsibility of a person based on anthropological data becomes an economic constraint. In other words, utility depends on rights and obligations, and therefore on the responsibility that is placed on each person. Faced with an anthropological obligation, the person can use economic methods; for example the theory or economic calculus. The person can manipulate information about income or compensate for a community obligation, such as donating goods rather than time to the community.

Substitutions are possible as part of a strategy. This substitution can be illustrated by classical microeconomic representations: indifference curves and Edgeworth boxes (Figure 2.1).

The time allocation will thus be particularly distorted by the time constraints linked to rights and obligations with anthropological priority rules. Economic theory retains a major choice between work and leisure within the time allocation. Community time plays a fundamental role between the two; for example, training children is neither a hobby nor a job, it typically corresponds to a community obligation.

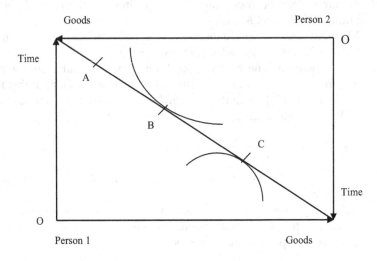

Figure 2.1 Imbalance between reciprocal obligations.

The community is a comprehensive entity; its value depends on its configuration (size, number of standards, quality of the corpus of standards, efficiency of the community).

The mechanism can be simplified (if not exaggerated) as follows (Figure 2.2):

- if the demand for social protection increases, the size of the community increases;
- if the size of the communities increases, the number of R/O norms must increase proportionally;
- if the number of R/O norms increases, the quality of the corpus of R/O norms decreases (standards become contradictory, their scope is diluted, etc.);
- ultimately, the efficiency of the R/O system (efficiency of the community) decreases and the demand for social protection is greater.

Behaviour in relation to time is a function of both selfish (intertemporal) disturbances and community disturbances, largely intergenerational, either upward or downward (Figure 2.3).

Figure 2.3 expresses the "interest rate" on an anthropological basis, depending on how each person feels about time. In the event of additional community pressure, the disturbances increase, the corresponding curve

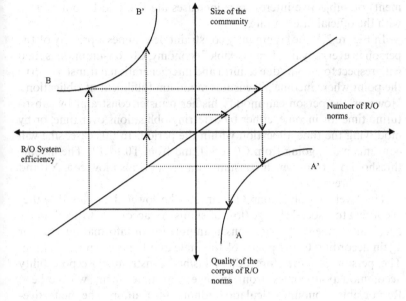

Figure 2.2 The community structure.

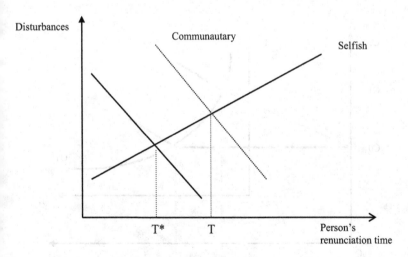

Figure 2.3 An anthropological treatment of economic time.

is higher; as a result, the renunciation of time (consumption, investment) or subjective interest rate increases are likely to be out of step with the official interest rate.

In Figure 2.4, the community constraint determines a priority of the person in everyday life. In a "flexible" economy, C0 consumption is rigid with respect to income due to intra and intergenerational transfers, up to the point where income Y0 ensures minimum fulfilment of obligations. However, the person can modify his/her transfer constraint by substituting time for income, either by deferring obligations over time, or by modifying the time allocation within the period. In this case, s/he will consume more, going from C0 to C1 and from T0 to T1. The income threshold Y1 from which consumption grows is also lowered; Y1 and Y0 are "thresholds".

The level of obligations O1 can still be lowered or raised, either according to a social change (loss of status), or according to a voluntary act (abandonment of obligations, manipulation of information, etc.), or again according to the policy of the State and the economic situation. The person can therefore adjust his/her constraints. Responsibility accommodation comes from income and time spent with others. Responsible economic calculation admits substitution. The ineffectiveness of economic policies then depends on the configuration of society, in particular, personal constraints on assets and time allocations. These

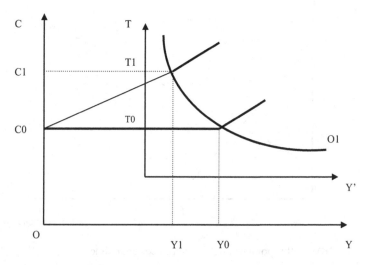

Figure 2.4 Priority and personal consumption.

constraints are all the stronger as the State withdraws in favour of personal responsibilities and these are aggravated by a strong social crisis (poverty, unemployment, family crises).

The economist assumes the data as objectively as possible; s/he has to deal with the problems of profitability that stand in the way of objectivity. There is a temptation to use extrapolated data for many years or to produce aggregate data from light surveys. Statistical ethics also concerns the treatment of the interviewee, in particular his remuneration. Statistical ethics implies that the economist integrates the different stages of his investigation, from the pre-investigation through to the analysis. We must avoid the relationship being built on a division of labour between data collectors in the South and analysts in the North, the main beneficiaries.[3]

A final example of the importance of the method relates to randomization, which is considered objective, but which depends on an anthropological context.

The method of economic anthropology is the synthesis of anthropological methods and economic methods. The structure of the person experiences vulnerabilities (economic) and suffering (anthropological).

Conclusion

The association of anthropology with economic thinking poses many problems. The economy is rather hypothetico-deductive. Anthropology is essentially based on a principle of reality and therefore is closer to sociology. Beyond that, economic ethics is based on two principles according to Arrow (1963), individualism and hedonism. It applies a double assumption of continuity and positive behaviour.

This economic anthropology admits the priority of the person and therefore a discontinuity; the person who fits both in a personal calculation and in taking others into account. It "understands" human phenomena before any systematic explanation. It is a phenomenology of the person. As such, it admits negative behaviour.

Economic anthropology has confined itself to the study of primitive societies and to conflicts of method. It is possible to revisit the association of anthropology with economics. The demands of economic anthropology, for example, the return to fieldwork and to human phenomena, would allow a phenomenology of the person.

This chapter has summarized the method of economic anthropology; a method which conditions the quality of economic data by taking into account the diversity of companies. This method accompanies the analysis but does not reject it.

Notes

1   Coordinate comparisons are studied with Suppes (1966) and S.C. Kolm (1972). See again Sen (1970) who develops the "Suppes's norm". This notion of coordinality is present in the economy of envy, notably in Varian (1974), who equates envy with the Rawlsian conception of resentment.
2   Veblen was highly criticized by economists, but at the same time he published in the biggest economic journals: JPE, QJE, REP. His positions on physical anthropology marginalized him, but eugenics and ethnic comparatism were often used by economists, like the founder of political economy, William Petty, with his scales of creatures human beings and his Californian weddings. This anthropology is treated in Mahieu (2001).
3   This desire for integration has resulted in the creation of a Master's degree in statistics applied to development, at ENSEA in Abidjan.

References

Akerlof, G.A., 1984, "The Market for Lemons, Quality, Uncertainty and the Market Mechanism", *The Quarterly Journal of Economics*, 84, 3: 488–500.

Arendt, H., 1958, *Condition de l'homme moderne*, Paris: Agora.

Arrow, K.J., 1963, *Social Choice and Individual Values*, 2nd edition, Cowles Foundation for Research in Economics at Yale University, New Haven and London: Yale UP.

Bardhan, P., 1993, "Economics of Development and the Development of Economics", *Journal of Economic Perspectives*, 7, 2: 129–142.

Barro, R., 1974, "Are Government Bonds Net Wealth?", *Journal of Political Economy*, 82, 6: 1095–1117.

Becker, G., 1974, "A Theory of Social Interactions", *Journal of Political Economy*, 82, 6: 1063–1093.

Buchanan, J.M., 1975, "The Samaritan's Dilemma", in E.S. Phelps (ed.), *Altruism, Morality and Economic Theory*, New York: Russel Sage Foundation, 71–75.

Clower, R., 1970, *Monetary Theory*, Baltimore: Penguin Books.

Gastellu, J.M., 1984, "Le droit à l'économie poétique", *Approche anthropologique et recherche économique à l'ORSTOM*, Journées d'étude, 13 et 14 décembre 1984, Collection Colloques et Séminaires, éditions de l'ORSTOM.

Geertz, C., 1996, *Ici et là-bas, l'anthropologue comme auteur*, Paris: Metai.

Godelier, M., 1974, *Un domaine contesté: l'anthropologie économique*, Paris: Mouton.

Goulet, D., 1965, *Etica del Desarrollo, Guia Teorica y Practica*, Barcelone: Estela/ IEPAL.

Harsanyi, J.C., 1995, "A Theory of Prudential Values and A Rule Utilitarian Theory of Morality", *Social Choice and Welfare*, 12, 4: 319–333.

Hayek, F.A., 1960, *The Constitution of Liberty*, London: Routledge & Kegan.

Kluckhohn, C., 1985, *Mirror for Man. The Relation of Anthropology to Modern Life*, Tucson: University of Arizona Press.

Kolm, S.C., 1972, *Justice et équité*, Paris: Edition du CNRS.

Lebret, L.J., 1968, *L'économie au service des hommes*, Paris: Editions du Cerf.

Lévi-Strauss, C., 1958, *Anthropologie structurale*, Paris: Plon.

Mahieu, F.R., 2001, *Ethique économique. Fondements anthropologiques*, Paris: L'Harmattan, Bibliothèque du Développement.

Malinvaud, E., 1991, *Voies de la recherche macroéconomique*, Paris: Odile Jacob.

Marshall, A., 1890, *Principles of Economics*, London: McMillan.

Mauss, M., 1950, *Sociologie et anthropologie*, Paris: PUF, Quadrige.

Myrdal, G., 1953, *The Political Element in the Development of Economic Theory*, London: Routledge & Kegan.

Roheim, G., 1978, *Psychanalyse et anthropologie: culture, personnalité, inconscient*, Paris: Gallimard.

Sahlins, M., 1972, *Age de pierre, âge d'abondance: l'économie des sociétés primitives*, Paris: Gallimard.

Simmel, G., 1991, *Secret et sociétés secrètes*, Strasbourg: Circé.

Spencer, H., 1891, *The Principles of Ethics*, réedit. Indianapolis: Liberty Classics.

Sraffa, P., 1970, *Production de marchandises par des marchandises*, Paris: Dunod.

Suppes, P., 1966, "Some Models of Grading Principles", *Synthèse*, 16: 184–306.

Tolstoï, L., 1892, "A propos du recensement de Moscou", réédité dans *L'argent et le travail*, Paris: Edition des Syrtes, 2007.

Vacher de Lapouge de, G., 1897, "The Fundamentals Laws of Anthropology", *Journal of Political Economy*, 6, 1: 54–92.

Varian, H.R., 1974, "Equity, Envy and Efficiency", *Journal of Economic Theory*, 9: 63–91.

Veblen, T., 1970, *Théorie de la classe de loisirs* (1899), Paris: Gallimard-Tel.

Von Mises, L., 1949, *Human Action, A Treatise on Economics*, London: W. Hodge & Co.

Weber, M., 1992, *Essais sur la théorie de la science*, Paris: Agora.

3 Integration of personal responsibility

Everyone is immersed in a community of rights and obligations that s/he can rationally order, trying not to offend his/her environment. S/he sequentially resolves his/her responsibility and then takes on the dimension of a person, responsible, rational, and reasonable. The debate on this attribution is very lively between the partisans of an *ex ante* responsibility and those who calculate this responsibility *ex post*.

In addition, we must also distinguish between intergenerational and intragenerational responsibility, the first more social, the second more environmental; social upheavals opposing ecological conservatism.

3.1 Responsibility

Personal responsibility, like economic anthropology, is the subject of much debate. Advocates of *ex ante* responsibility, infinite in time and space, oppose those of *ex post* responsibility.

3.1.1 Definition

Responsibility is understood at three levels: obligation, imputation, sanction.[1] A person stands up for another person (or himself/herself) so that action is taken and bears the consequences. Simply put, an obligation to perform an action is assimilated to a responsibility to perform this action. This obligation is attributed to a given person (see the importance of the imputation capacity in Ricoeur's work). Finally, failure to comply with an obligation is accompanied by sanctions. Assuming this constraint is constitutive of the person and of freedom; the sequence of first freedom, the use of which is judged by a responsibility as accountability (Roemer, 1996), is an alternative to the responsibility of the person. Responsibility is conceived in a totally different way, *a posteriori* in a natural society with opportunistic individuals

DOI: 10.4324/9781003386742-4

and *a priori* in a legal society with people. The ethics of responsibility asserts, according to Max Weber (1992), that: "*We must answer for the foreseeable consequences of our actions*". But in front of who?

Responsibility is a motivation that has very different contents, many forms (guarantee, obligation, guilt, etc.). It can be a virtue or a vice depending on the context. There is currently a strong opposition between the phenomenology of responsibility and responsibility conceived as a cause-and-effect relationship within the framework of the theory of action. Hence, we distinguish the moral responsibility attached to the person in relation to others for a given action, and the more impersonal responsibility linked to the action for given individuals. The moral responsibility of the person is immense in the conceptions of a duty in relation to any other person or to all future generations. This is a potential and prospective liability.

This *a priori* "ascription" attributes rights and obligations to a person according to his/her identity and his/her history. For example, his/her family rank (elder or younger) and professional status will determine the extent of his/her responsibility.

Responsibility, according to Jonas, characterizes the person beyond the individual. Anthropologically, the person is differentiated from the individual, "*it is the only being known to us who can have a responsibility*" (Jonas, 1998). This ability to identify oneself and to speak primarily differentiates the person from beings, and therefore primarily between people. The responsibility could be infinite in time (Jonas, 1979) and in space (Levinas, 1989); however, it is limited by each person, according to his/her means and feelings. Each person is thus able to constrain himself/herself within certain limits.

There are many ways of dealing with responsibility in moral philosophy and in politics today. The approach chosen here is the positive ethics of the person in relation to his/her "community".[2] It analyses how an individual responsible for himself and others, manages his rights and especially his obligations. This ethics has a limited scope compared to philosophy, but taken seriously by economists, changes radically the utopian hypothesis of a "free individual", a fiction that determines microeconomics. This conception, inherited by economists from the Enlightenment philosophy, underestimates the capacity of the individual to restrain himself and to be a responsible person. Economics is a hypothetical social science and nothing prevents one from changing the assumptions. The responsible person replaces the opportunistic individual; s/he assumes a sequence: responsibility → rationality → reasonability.

From lived and conscious experience, from fieldwork study, phenomena arise. Transfers and health create discussions; are they subject to prior constraint or individual insurance?

These human experiences appear through signals, for example, suicide. The existential problem of community constraints is important. Freedom lies in this ability to assume responsibility. Responsibility determines freedom, contrary to the idea of philosophical radicalism, in particular Sen (1993), which makes responsibility for freedom as accounting dependent on its use.

Responsibility → Freedom (Phenomenology)
Freedom → Responsibility (Radicalism)

Ethics, for example of responsibility, is conceived *a priori*, unlike accountability in Sen for whom responsibility is *ex post* and depends on the use that the individual makes of his freedom. The positions of Levinas (1972) and Jonas (1979) on this priority are very strong. Each person has an infinite responsibility in time and space. We see, with Ricoeur,[3] the importance of the capacities of the person, to assume responsibility. This ethics is positive; it describes behaviours if not deconstructs them (Derrida, 1967; Bataille, 1980). It observes the behaviour of the responsible person, unlike personalism (Mounier, 1971) which is normative. The person is social and responsible, has an ethical priority, and is capable of self-restraint (Rousseau, 1755; Kant, 1797).

3.1.2 An application: personal rights and obligations

Human experience reveals a world of rights and obligations, an *a priori* responsibility. The analysis is synchronic rather than diachronic, looking for the rights and obligations of a person at a given point in time. However, this external constraint does not invalidate the idea of a freedom assumed by self-constraint. Two forms of economic calculation can be distinguished regarding a good X (individual) and a good Y (personal).[4]

Utilitarianism:

Utility → individual → X → supply / demand → market price / partial equilibrium → general equilibrium.

Phenomenology:

Responsibility → person → Y → obligations / rights → esteem of the community → society's equilibrium.

Each person can react rationally by playing on the components of this responsibility, and also by playing on the corresponding information, going so far as to refuse promotions so as not to increase community pressure. But we must remain reasonable vis-à-vis the community so as not to be excluded, suffer a paranoid neurosis, and become a social orphan. This reasonability towards the community is part of Rawls's self-criticism, but this is not retained by Amartya Sen. According to Freud, it illustrates the substitution of the power of the community over the freedom of the individual.

Responsibility → Rationality → Reasonability

The subject has a capacity structure (Ricoeur, 1983) and his/her possible suffering arises from a loss of capacities. This subject thus defined is a person, a totality structured in capacities, capable of imputing responsibility to himself/herself. Hence the importance of his/her identity structure, by articulating several kinds of total interpretation, the object of hermeneutics (Gadamer, 1960). It replaces humankind with his/her constraints in his/her everyday life, including his/her capacity for self-restraint as a condition of his/her freedom; instead of denying it any moral or religious influence. Faced with the phenomenon of *inter vivos* transfers, the error of the experts was to immediately resort to a standard theory of voluntary insurance, without seeking to understand the nature and intensity of the constraints which are sources of vulnerability for the people concerned.

Freedom can only be understood through sequence, community constraint → rationality → reasonability; a sequence highlighted by economic anthropology and which emphasizes the initial hypotheses of economic phenomenology about the person, responsible and vulnerable.

3.1.3 *The community, place of responsibility*

Each person assumes a set of rights and obligations vis-à-vis his/her community. Obligations translate economically into resource constraints and time constraints. In many cases, asset and time constraints are substitutable for a given level of obligations; the absence during an important manifestation of social life will be compensated by a monetary transfer, otherwise the inability to give a sum of money will be replaced by time, possibly supplemented by material reparation. Indifference curves can therefore be used, each curve expressing a given level of obligations for a person. This indifference curve expresses the potential goods/time substitutability for an individual (Figure 3.1). The effective balance will

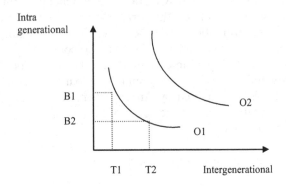

Figure 3.1 The conflict of responsibilities.

be a function of the community preference in relation to goods, time, and the material situation of the national.

The calculation of my rights and my obligations (R/O) depends on societal or local standards which show community pressure. This pressure can be likened to a voluntary exchange if the fact of assuming my R/O expresses my freedom (cf. Rousseau, Kant). The utility is therefore endogenized and results from my calculation of R/O. The person is not only responsible but compels himself/herself. Responsibility expresses the rights and obligations of a person of a given social status. It is not automatically realized, like any deontic expression.[5]

The individual situation in terms of rights and obligations can be represented by a graph distinguishing on an abscissa the rights and obligations according to their intensity, and on an ordinate their distribution in time (Figure 3.2). Liability is potential and will become effective as a response to a request.[6]

This responsibility can be strong (an obligation or a prohibition, of an ethical nature) or weak (a possibility/necessity, alethically). It can be purely moral or accompanied by sanctions (e.g. the guarantee).

3.2 Rationality

There are several ways that a person under community pressure can react, specifically by concealing his/her characteristics. Leximin is such a subterfuge that the "richest of the rich" prioritize the "poorest of the poor" with the smallest sacrifice; the disproportion ensures that this redistribution does not infringe on freedom. The donor can hide his

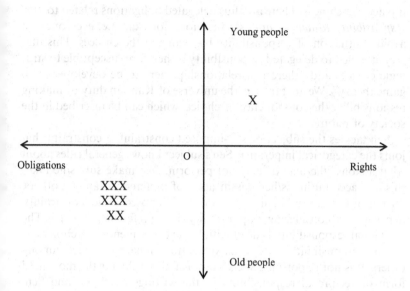

Figure 3.2 Map of rights and obligations.

social status, deny his income, overestimate his obligations already fulfilled, etc.

Knowing my moral responsibility, my rights and my obligations, it is advisable to make a rational choice according to my interests; for example, prioritizing my obligations by trying to reconcile logic and morality. It is my responsibility to make this choice, even if it means making a metalogical decision between the norms. Here, the principle of accountability follows freedom of choice. How did I use my freedom, given my handicaps and my merits? What was my capacity of choice[7] (agency)? This rationality can be expressed by a choice on the persons and also, on the modalities of the responsibility; I can play on time, property, affection, etc., for a given level of responsibility. Rather, it lies in the theory of action, either direct or indirect.

What is important is the consistency of the choice; for example, how to associate freedom and rationality (Arrow, 1963), or even freedom and Pareto-unanimity (Sen, 1970)? How did I abuse this prerogative or not? I have to give an account of it to myself and to others. There is direct and indirect responsibility because I can entrust this choice to people I trust. On this occasion a weakened version of responsibility appears in Sen (2005) with fiduciary responsibility and a corresponding "dignity". In fact, it is about delegated responsibility and the constraint it places on choices. There are thus delegated obligations related to "*the responsibility to act for other*s"; therefore, for example, everyone can avoid a situation of responsibility by changing the choices. This dignity attached to delegated responsibility is therefore susceptible to strategic choices and "there is a relationship there to be developed with game theory". We are far from the universe of Kantian duty by making responsibility the consequence of choice, which can be inscribed in the society of nature.

Sen tackles the subject of self-imposed constraint, a constraint that joins the categorical imperative. Sen's subject knows general rules about what actions s/he may or may not perform. Just make sure s/he takes this into account in his/her classification of preferences (among others, on acts of choice) and in his/her way of self-imposed choice constraints. Sen suggests considering responsibility as a preference, "as if". The individual responsibility is dealt with by its consequences on choices.

This responsibility is only a maximization on narrow choices among others. It is not important. Social responsibility is by far the most used form of reciprocal responsibility in the writings of Rawls and Sen. Society is responsible for a certain political freedom and citizens are responsible for the democratic quality of society through the use they make of it. We are there in a context of positive freedom, very far from Kant's self-restraint.

3.3 Reasonability

This responsibility is much more complex than the previous one, given the relationship between the person and the "community". People must account for their behavior according to their interpersonal relationships, in particular the expectations of the people concerned, regarding them. The person in Rawls's work appears after 1971; to the priority of the Just over the Good has juxtaposed that of the Reasonable (the ability to abstract oneself from one's interests) over the Rational (in the sense of neoclassical theory): "*The members of society are conceived not only as rational individuals, but as legal persons who can cooperate for mutual benefit*".

The reasonable person can fail, emphasizing the ambivalent nature of responsibility which is not "good in itself". In the name of my calculating responsibility, I can decide not to transfer anything and dismiss the beggars. But if I behave badly in relation to my home community, sanctions are possible, at least self-suggested. I make a choice under the "veil of ignorance" (Rawls, 1971) of my interests and seek consensus. I establish myself as the person who instigates the action and leads it to its consequences on the agency of the community. I am challenged by my community which asks me to answer for my choices.

I am responsible to my community for action under the constraint of sanctions for me and the community for a deadline. This responsibility towards the community can take several occurrences: being active, inactive, accomplished, postponed, rejected, violated, etc. A simulation is therefore possible on agents,[8] but everything depends on their nature: individuals of natural society or people of a community of rights and obligations. Responsibility to the community is a constraint that weighs on people and can be exorbitant. So, some "officials" have no choice, given community sanctions; they have to endure community pressures beyond their means.[9] The relation between these three terms can be represented according to Figure 3.3 expressing my inner freedom.

Responsibility increases in proportion to the size of the community and the number of obligations. A minimum of responsibility depends on the rationality of the means, a maximum corresponds to reasonability. A position of balance can be point E, intermediate between rigour and laxity: it expresses the inner freedom of the person. The question becomes more complicated with the information the person has about his/her perception by the community.

How is the altruism of the community in relation to a person? This can be in complete asymmetry of information: it is persuaded to do Good, but the community perceives it as Evil. This situation means

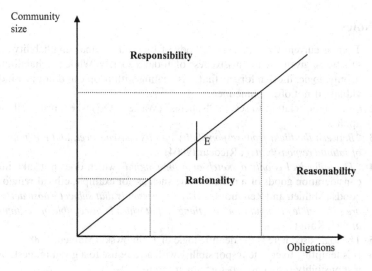

Figure 3.3 The responsibility between reasonability and rationality.

that reasonability can be situated in a context of risk or uncertainty. The community has accumulated social capital[10] in relation to a person and this can be positive, neutral, or negative. It is therefore essential for a person to obtain information on his/her perception by the community, hence traditional or modern "clinics" and the corresponding costs. The community is a club (Buchanan, 1975) divided between several imperatives: size, efficiency, benevolence. It can be benevolent and effective in a first configuration, malicious and ineffective in other cases. It is, contrary to some communalist views, never "good" in itself.

Conclusion

An anthropological approach to economics involves changing the subject, from the individual to the person.

This person is immersed in a world of rights and obligations that pre-exists the pursuit of happiness. The permanent watch (the infinite responsibility) of each person on his/her community determines his/her economic acts, by the gains or losses inherent in the various responsibilities.

The person appears with the "exercise" of responsibility and not just being responsible. His/her responsibility is immediate and disproportionate. There is a growing conflict between social responsibility, intragenerational, and environmental responsibility, intergenerational. Ecological conservatism opposes social upheaval.

Notes

1 There is currently a considerable body of literature formalizing liability and sanctions, given the permissiveness of today's society. While it rehabilitates deontic logic, it often forgets that it is dealing with people and not just individuals, if not of machine-men.
2 Or again in relation to several "spheres" (Walzer, 1983) where responsibility applies.
3 "*Between the flight from responsibility and its consequences, and the inflation of infinite responsibility*", Ricoeur (2004).
4 "*The individual is only a sketch of a humankind*" which does not take into consideration goods of a moral nature such as, for example, ethical-religious goods (Mahieu and Zemmour, 2010). "*A person is that subject whose actions are susceptible of imputation, the thing is that which is susceptible of no imputation*", Kant (1797).
5 The logic used here is the deontic logic of Kalinowski (Mahieu, 1988).
6 It is tempting to equate responsibility with a response to a given request, but responsibility is potential before any response.

7 This responsibility relates mainly to myself, it will be judged rather selfish.
8 A considerable literature performs simulations on this type of formulation, mainly to assess how to strengthen standards and sanctions.
9 In a survey of civil servants in Daoukro, Ivory Coast (Mahieu and Odunfa, 1989), a third of them endure community pressure greater than their income.
10 See Ballet and Mahieu (2003).

References

Arrow, K.J., 1963, *Social Choice and Individual Values*, 2nd edition, Cowles Foundation for Research in Economics at Yale University, New Haven and London: Yale University Press.

Ballet, J., Mahieu, F.R., 2003, "Le capital social, mesure et incertitude du rendement", in J. Ballet and R. Guillon (eds), *Regards croisés sur le capital social*, Paris: L'Harmattan, 41–56.

Bataille, G., 1980, *La part maudite*, Paris: Les Éditions de Minuit.

Buchanan, J.M., 1975, "The Samaritan's Dilemma", in E.S. Phelps (ed.), *Altruism, Morality and Economic Theory*, New York: Russel Sage Foundation, 71–75.

Derrida, J., 1967, *L'écriture et la différence*, Paris: Editions du Seuil.

Gadamer, H.G., 1960, *Vérité et Méthode*, Paris: PUF.

Jonas, H., 1979, *Le principe responsabilité: une éthique pour la civilisation technologique*, Paris: Editions du Cerf.

Jonas, H., 1998, *Pour une éthique du futur*, Paris: Payot.

Kant, E., 1994, *Métaphysique des mœurs II. Doctrine du droit. Doctrine de la vertu (1797)*, Paris: GF-Flammarion.

Levinas, E., 1972, *Humanisme de l'autre homme*, Paris: Le Livre de Poche, Biblio Essais, 1987.

Levinas, E., 1989, *Le temps et l'autre*, Paris: Quadrige-PUF.

Mahieu, F.R., 1988, *Logique déductive et théorie économique*, Abidjan: PUSAF/ Paris: L'Harmattan.

Mahieu, F.R., Odunfa, A., 1989, "Droits et obligations à Daoukro, Côte d'Ivoire", *Miméo, Séminaire d'économie publique*, Université d'Abidjan.

Mahieu, F.R., Zemmour, M., 2010, "Ethiques de la vertu et de la religion face au développement durable", *FREE*, Journée Ethique, juin, http://ethique. perso.sfr.fr/zemourmahieu.pdf

Mounier, E., 1971, *Le personnalisme*, Paris: PUF.

Rawls, J., 1971, *A Theory of Justice*, The Belknap Press, Harvard University.

Ricoeur, P., 1983, *Temps et récits I*, Paris: Editions du Seuil.

Ricoeur, P., 2004, *Parcours de la reconnaissance*, Paris: Stock.

Roemer, J., 1996, *Egalitarian Perspectives, Essays in Philosophical Economics*, Cambridge, UK: Cambridge U. Press.

Rousseau, J.J., 1992, "Discours sur l'économie politique", *Ecrits politiques (1755)*, Paris: Livre de Poche.

Sen, A.K., 1970, *Collective Choice and Social Welfare*, San Fransisco: Holden-Day.
Sen, A.K., 1993, *Ethique et économie*, Paris: PUF.
Sen, A.K., 2005, *La démocratie des autres*, Paris: Payot.
Walzer, M., 1983, *Spheres of Justice*, London: Basic Books.
Weber, M., 1992, *Essais sur la théorie de la science*, Paris: Agora.

4 An anthropology of human and social vulnerability

Vulnerability originally refers to the possibility of a human being injured if not killed. This is not a new notion in philosophy and in social sciences. Basic concept, analogous to fragility in Ricoeur's philosophy (Ricoeur, 1988), vulnerability is very precise in social economy: vulnerability at work, unemployment, poverty, harassment, etc.

On the other hand, the extension of this notion to social groups and countries is recent. Thus, economists have integrated vulnerability into macroeconomics, in particular, to illustrate economies exposed to shocks. The International Monetary Fund retains global indicators relating to a nation's macroeconomic vulnerability: debt, liquidity, reserves, corporate performance. This vulnerability considered at aggregate level is very far from the human dimension. The use of the notion of vulnerability is expanding without the concept being well defined. The World Bank states that *"vulnerability measures the likelihood of a shock leading to a decline in well-being"*. However, vulnerability can occur without probability and if it is probable, not be measurable. On the other hand, by being based on probabilities, vulnerability cannot escape the debate between objective and subjective probability.

Several authors, G. Shackle (1949), J. Hicks (1965), question the capacity of probabilities to integrate "possibilities" or even "potential surprises" of a person in relation to events. Hicks says the likelihood of disaster cannot be measured. According to Shackle, vulnerability is a loss of control over events. Ultimately, probability would be a *"reflection of our ignorance"* (Suppes, 1966), commensurate with events such as epidemics, volcanic eruptions, major storms, earthquakes, and so on. These are plausible but not probable events; which poses serious problems of reparation and is currently giving rise to a debate on the nature of compensation. This debate shows the need to broaden the field of methods related to the formalization of the vulnerability of the person, by distinguishing different modalities of probability,

DOI: 10.4324/9781003386742-5

possibility, or plausibility, but also to reframe conceptually and sequentially the vulnerability in relation to the fragility, fallibility, or even "faultivity".

This double opening of vulnerability, at the levels of method and concepts, is the subject of this chapter. It is organized as follows.

Firstly, we define vulnerability and we show the reasons why it is difficult to give a precise definition, then we introduce the notions of fragility and fallibility.

Secondly, we combine the notion of responsibility with that of vulnerability. Responsibility allows us to analyse the vulnerability of the person through the example of *inter vivos* transfers and pluriactivity.

Thirdly, we discuss the measurement of vulnerability by probabilities. We show that probability is not effective in measuring vulnerability given that the person is not only vulnerable, but also fragile and fallible. Therefore, policies to fight poverty, for example, must take into account the fragility and fallibility of the person.

Finally in the last section we present our main conclusions.

4.1 Define vulnerability

Human and social vulnerability is studied here at the level of the responsible person. The person suffers like any individual from events that weaken him/herself, but in addition, his/her vulnerability is accentuated by the weight (the disproportion) of responsibilities. Vulnerability translates for the person by an attack on his/her agency, his/her capacity to act and react to events, in particular, by a destabilization of the structure of his/her capacities. Sustainable human development involves ascendency over events to avoid permanent, transitory, or cyclical vulnerability.

4.1.1 A difficult definition

Vulnerability covers various periods when a person's situation (the disproportion of his/her obligations) or the evolution of his/her environment (disappearance of protections) reduces his/her capacity to protect or to react to hazards (risk or uncertain). Vulnerability can be permanent, transitory, if not cyclical, so it is very dependent on temporal modalities. On the other hand, it is partial (vulnerability to unemployment) or general (vulnerability to poverty) for a given person. In other words, vulnerability is a particular critical situation of exposure to a risk of "injury" (poverty, unemployment, disease, conflict, indignity, exclusion, etc.), therefore to a negative event. Policies can destroy some defences, which provided invulnerability. Thus, an anti-poverty policy can create vulnerability. For example, in very poor countries, we transform (through ill-conceived food or financial aid) miserable pluriactive farmers into poorly trained artisans, who, without a corresponding market, are weakened or vulnerable and unable to use their pluriactivity. The sustainability of anti-poverty policies depends in large part on this question: won't improving social indicators lead to even greater vulnerability?

Vulnerability results in a destabilization of the structure of activities, income, and capacities. Vulnerability is a particular fragility (exposure) of a person to a factor (demography, economic policy, self-restraint, responsibility) which destabilizes his/her ability to protect himself/herself and therefore his/her influence over events. A person vulnerable to poverty is not immediately poor, but may fall back into poverty more strongly, relative to time and others. So, this is a particular fragility and results in a strong possibility of falling or relapsing into a given misfortune.

Fragility is very different according to the subjects studied, individual, person, citizen, agent, etc., the angle of vision, micro, meso or macroeconomic and especially according to the temporal modality. Sustainable development must combine intragenerational vulnerabilities, in the short and medium term, with those which are intergenerational (long term). There are cyclical vulnerabilities and structural vulnerabilities. The malnourished and abused child experiences a structural vulnerability, for example, the person can be abandoned as a "child sorcerer" (Ballet and Mahieu, 2009). Yet some people can go through a difficult phase and get over it for good. We can thus distinguish a strong vulnerability (irremediable) from a weak vulnerability (remediable); but also, the vulnerability "in oneself" (unconscious) of that "for oneself" (conscious).

Vulnerability has a particular meaning in bioethics in the form of a vulnerability principle. This principle prescribes *"respect, concern and protection of others and of living things in general, on the basis of the universal observation of the fragility, finitude and mortality of others"* (Hottois and Missa, 2001).

Responsibility and vulnerability are two principles associated with the person. Vulnerability concerns all areas of life and in the economy, all possible areas: production, consumption, savings, investment. Fragility designates, according to Ricoeur, the disproportion linked to the responsibility of the person. As this dimension of the subject (the responsible person) is barely addressed, it will be explored in the following points.

4.1.2   *Vulnerability, fragility, fallibility, faultivity*

In a human conception of economics, subjects are laden with responsibility and therefore vulnerable and fallible; the disproportion of responsibilities makes them vulnerable and can lead them to error.

Indeed, responsibility like altruism is not good in itself. It can turn out to be malicious and criminal. Selfish hedonism responds to a broader conception of values, in the name of a positive conception of ethics.

Ultimately, economic radicalism views individuals as objects, unlike economic anthropology which takes them as subjects responsible for their destiny. The individual as an object is not free; he obeys his instincts and fatal laws. The autonomous person, capable of being responsible, assumes his/her choices and constraints, thereby proving his/her freedom. Overloaded with responsibilities, possibly contradictory, threatened with sanctions, everyone is vulnerable. S/he may find himself/herself confused about having to choose; for example, the head of the family in complete poverty will resort to stealing. Responsibility thus leads to fault. My political engagement leads me to kill my best friend.[1]

Paul Ricoeur (1995) insists on the "disproportion" which makes the person capable of failing. Thus, the sequence of responsibilities can end with a capability[2] to do evil. Fallibility is an ambiguous concept for Ricoeur; it expresses both error (cf. the infallibility of the Pope) and the propensity to do harm. This double meaning poses a problem of consistency insofar as evil can follow an infallible process. The rationality of evil, of crime for example, is the subject of an economic theory (Becker, 1974) which claims to be a-moral. It is therefore necessary to dissociate fallibility from the faulty capacity to do harm. This propensity for fault can be expressed by faultivity. The error in relation to the project of humanity makes the responsible capable of a fault in the sense of an injury to the person. Faultivity is a negative capacity or even capability, a freedom to harm oneself and/or others. Ricoeur states "*the constitutional weakness which makes evil possible*". Faultivity evokes a negative capability, the freedom to do evil. The disproportion can be internal (relative to the weight of obligations versus resources) or external (intragenerational versus intergenerational).

Vulnerability or fragility accounts for the destruction of the person risk. Are the human costs generated by development humanly sustainable?

The Perroux-style human costs are the social levels that must be ensured for humans. Responsibility in economics can be simplified by likening it to an initial pressure (r) on income, Y; let rY, where Yd the disposable income is $Yd = (1 - r)Y$, rY is a threshold of responsibility if $Y < rY$, then the person becomes vulnerable and fallible. The threshold is no longer a physiological minimum, but a minimum capacity to be responsible, to constrain oneself. This threshold induces reactions in the event of questioning and random effects.

With disposable income, a person can freely choose how to act around consumption and investment. There is thus an initial capacity to fulfil his/her obligations which conditions the later choice of the person between the uses of income. In other words, the ability to assume one's responsibilities conditions capability as a rational free choice. The problem of responsibility goes beyond that of nominal income level, but depends on r. A person with a high income can be under a strong constraint of responsibility and conversely a poor person can benefit from a strong support, blurring the poverty lines. This liability threshold is therefore very variable depending on the social situation of each person.

4.2 Vulnerability and responsibility

Vulnerability is a function that relates to two variables, one designating the person and the other the domain or action giving rise to this vulnerability. The most frequently cited areas relate to health, employment, altruism. Responsibility is one of the least studied areas of vulnerability.

4.2.1 A special case: the person responsible is therefore vulnerable

Each person has capacities that s/he can use, in the face of his/her economic constraints, to live in a state of well-being. Deprivation of these capacities, which are mainly "real",[3] defines capacity poverty. Capacities take many forms (economic, human, social, financial, etc.), with monetary income being only one component of these capabilities. Since the person is not an "irrational idiot" (Sen, 1993), s/he intelligently combines his/her capacities, playing on his/her properties and their limits, in order to assume his/her responsibilities while remaining reasonable towards his/her community. S/he can, for example, work more in his/her declared job, play on state subsidies, activate *inter vivos* transfers, have informal occupations, etc. This combination defines his/her capacity structure. This structure has an obvious interest: any combination of capacities, if it is well adapted to the context, makes the person less vulnerable to external shocks and, therefore, to the risk of falling into poverty. In addition, it increases his/her chances of getting out of it quickly in case of difficulties. This allows him/her to avoid poverty traps and, above all, the risk of locking up the children who are the next generation.

Experience shows that this structure remains relatively stable: the level of education, state of health, social network, ability to work, financial means, etc., vary only slightly in the short term. It is, nevertheless, fragile considering the limits which exist in the capacities considered in relation to each other. There are limits to paid work, transfers, informal activities, both individual and social. Therefore, the substitution between abilities also has its limits: salaried work can be replaced by private assistance, individual income by social income, but only within certain limits. These limits result in "threshold effects" beyond which the expected effects are thwarted. The capacity structure then risks becoming ineffective or even malicious, through perverse effects, and making the person even more vulnerable.

Poverty reduction measures, in each socioeconomic context, influence the capacity structure of the people concerned. As long as the capacity limits are not reached, the capacity structure rebuilds itself in such a way as to reduce the vulnerability of the person. Nevertheless, and paradoxically, this structure can sometimes be destabilized, even if we wanted to strengthen all or part of the existing capacities. Hence the observation that social policies, against poverty or unemployment for example, can destroy capacities and strengthen the vulnerability of the people concerned. This is especially true for women who face a long *"chain of gender inequalities"*.[4] In this context, the limits in their capacity structures are narrower, due to time constraints and family responsibilities. To avoid increasing their vulnerability, perfectly tailored and targeted measures are needed that take into account existing capacity structures.

The destructuring of capacities is sometimes reversible after some time: thus, job loss, reduced income, temporary illness, social tensions can be overcome by the substitution, within certain limits, of one capacity for another. For example, the transition from the formal sector to the informal sector, to multi-activity, compensates, in terms of income, for the loss of a job, but it can also be irreversible; loss of health, inability to work, genocide, these are not reversible or compensable situations. In this case, a minimum of precaution is necessary.

In this context, humanly sustainable development will seek to strengthen capacity structures while preserving ("on average" and within "thresholds") the relationships between certain capacities. Development, through the structural changes it induces, inevitably leads to a change in capacities: for example, changes in social relations, a decline in social transfers, along with an improvement in individual income. However, a "stabilized" approach would require taking into account the fragility of the capacity structure and avoiding excessive short-term shocks to personal capacities. This requires a good knowledge of personal and social capacities, but also of adapted techniques.

4.2.2 *Representation and prediction tools*

The person has "freely" a structure of capacities (goods, time, altruism) in the face of the constraints of survival. The simplest form of this capacity is in economics, real cash,[5] and becomes more complex[6] with wealth, a risky asset structure. The result is a demand function for capacities or "development". This structure is vulnerable, given the limits of these capacities, considered in relation to each other. There are limits in paid work, transfers, informal activities for example, either individual or social. For example, solidarity has its limits beyond which it can generate social conflicts and self-destruction of this type of resource. Therefore, the substitution of capacities has obvious limits: wage labour can be replaced by private assistance, individual income by social income within certain limits. This can be represented by substitution boundaries within a capacity map according to the following diagram (Figure 4.1).

The *x*-axis represents formal income obtained through activity on the right side, and public transfers obtained through redistribution on the left side. Informal income from activities linked to social capital is represented on the *y*-axis, with the upper part of private *inter*

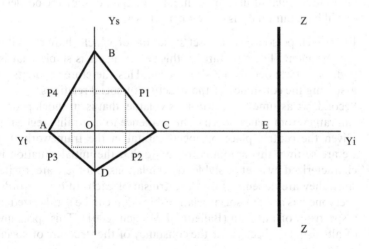

Figure 4.1 Structure of personal capacities.

vivos transfers and on the lower part the income obtained through an informal activity.

In this graph, the lines from one axis to another axis represent the frontier of potential capacities. Four types of borders are represented.

The upper part of the graph indicates the effects of direct substitution between capacities. Thus, on the northeast and northwest quadrants, it is possible to obtain more formal income against a fewer transfers, and more private transfers against fewer State transfers. State transfers supplement formal income. Rising formal income reduces transfers from others. Likewise, a society where State transfers are important may reduce private transfers.

The lower part of the graph indicates the indirect substitution effects linked to the time allocation. On the south-eastern quadrant, the individual chooses the distribution of his time between formal activity and informal activity. On the southwest quadrant, a substitution effect in time allocation also exists. For possible State aid, one can obtain a more or less, strong combination of State transfers and informal income. To the extent that public transfers are generally conditional, that is, they involve activities and procedures associated with the payment of these transfers, the time available for informal activity is reduced. An increase in State transfers then translates into lower informal income for a given set of combinations. The individual therefore chooses his time allocation and the distribution of his income, represented here by a point on the border, that is, points P1, P2, P3, P4. These points represent the situation of an individual at a given moment in time (we could add for each border an individual utility function, tangent at a point of the border).

We will base our analysis on two hypotheses.

• First, each person has an asset structure, of which share capital is a component. The structure of this set of assets is stable, that is, it does not change in the short term. This therefore amounts to assuming the constancy of the structure of social relations.

• Second, we assume that altruism is volatile; that is, in shock people can range from benevolence to malevolence to neutrality (egoism). Given the central place of social capital in the framework that we are setting, this amounts to saying that the initial situation is characterized by a set of stable social relations, but these are fragile, since they are dependent on the altruism of each. In other words, everyone has a set of social relationships that can be synthesized in a spectrum of altruism (Ballet and Mahieu, 2001). This spectrum of altruism has, because of the constancy of the structure of social relations, a structural form. However, due to the fragility of altruism, a shock to social capital, or more generally, to the asset structure, can lead to a cyclical distortion of this spectrum, for example, amplifying its malicious part. Under these conditions, any policy which will have the effect of modifying the composition of social capital or which will produce a modification of the structure of assets, risks causing a distortion of the spectrum of altruism and thus causes a loss of survival capacities of the individuals concerned.

Conclusion

Vulnerability is a typical notion of anthropology; it concerns people whose fragility is largely linked to economic variables. People, because of their responsibilities, experience increased vulnerability. Vulnerability results from disproportionalities in intra and intergenerational responsibilities.

Human and social vulnerability refers to the difficulties in which the people concerned find themselves, for example, discontinuities in consumption and work. Altruism can thus increase vulnerability and be negative. Altruism, social capital, can take on negative values along a multivalent spectrum.

Notes

1 Illustrated by Ken Loach's film, *The Wind That Shakes the Barley*; the Irish cause leads to shooting his best friends if not his own brother.
2 Capability defined in the sense of Sen.
3 In the economic sense of non-monetary and therefore evaluable by relative prices.
4 Dubois J-L. (2000).
5 The simplest expression is the ratio of money held to income corrected by prices, again the monetization coefficient, or $k = \dfrac{M}{pY}$. The capacity structure can be assessed as a composite stock or as a request for addition to this stock or "capacity demand". This demand is a function of the usefulness of the different forms of capacity: human, economic, social, financial, which can be assimilated to the demand for development. In an extensive conception of capacity, one can invent social, cultural, religious, symbolic capital, corresponding investments and income.
6 The short-term variation in capacities is very different depending on their nature; it is very small for education, it can be very large for health.

References

Ballet, J., Mahieu, F.R., 2001, "Entitlement Map and Social Capital as Capabilities Indicators", Paper, Justice and Poverty Colloquium, University of Cambridge, 5–7.

Ballet, J., Mahieu, F.R., 2009, "Capabilité et capacité dans le développement. Repenser la question du sujet dans l'œuvre d'Amartya Sen", *Tiers Monde*, 198: 303–316.

Becker, G., 1974, "A Theory of Social Interactions", *Journal of Political Economy*, 82, 6: 1063–1093.

Dubois, J-L., 2000, "Comment les politiques de lutte contre la pauvreté prennent-elles en compte les inégalités sexuées?", in Th. Locoh (ed.), *Genre, population et développement, les pays du Sud*, Paris: Dossiers et recherches de l'INED, 85.

Hicks, J., 1965, *Capital and Growth*, Oxford: Clarendon Press.

Hottois, G., Missa, J.N. (eds), 2001, *Nouvelle Encyclopédie de Bioéthique. Médecine-Environnement-Biotechnologie*, Louvain-La-Neuve: De Bœck Université.

Ricoeur, P., 1988, *Finitude et capabilité*, Paris: Editions du Seuil.

Ricoeur, P., 1995, *Le Juste*, Paris: Esprit.

Sen, A.K., 1993, *Ethique et économie*, Paris: PUF.

Shackle, G., 1949, *Expectations in Economics*, Cambridge: Cambridge University Press.

Suppes, P., 1966, "Some Models of Grading Principles", *Synthèse*, 16: 184–306.

5   The suffering of the person

The economy produces, beyond commodities, utility (positive or negative) and human suffering.[1] In particular, work *"in the effort, in its grief
and its pain"* (Levinas, 1989) builds the *"tragedy of loneliness"*. This
suffering appears through physical and mental deterioration, due, for
example, to working conditions or forced unemployment, to problems
with the living environment (lead, asbestos, poor housing), nutri-
tional errors, loss of solidarity, lack of recognition, discrimination, or
even fear.[2]

> *Indeed, it is in anguish and insecurity that modern man evolves in
> the world of work, with stagnant and uncertain wages, qualifications
> poorly recognized or insufficiently used, in jobs chosen by urgency or
> necessity, with the continuous threat of competition and unemploy-
> ment, these are the conditions that weaken the professional identity
> of man, with secret and very deep suffering.*
>
> (Behar, 1997)

From this point of view, the increase in suicides in certain companies
reflects maximum suffering. In the pursuit of standard well-being,
suffering is fatally marginalized, in the name of the belief that well-
being decreases suffering.

In many surveys devoted to the standard of living of poor households,
comments on suffering are classified off topic. In our societies, suffering
is often neglected, especially in its relation to death,[3] for example, there
is occupational medicine, but no unemployment medicine to study
its devastating consequences. Suffering also stems from the appropriation neurosis, a neurosis denounced by religions and great moral-
ities, for example, Buddhism.[4] The neuroses of society are expressed
by frustration, envy, aggressiveness (Nicolaï, 1999); they have dramatic

DOI: 10.4324/9781003386742-6

consequences for people in a competitive system, with its share of harassment and suffering.

Can the economy compensate for suffering? Conversely, is "resilience" (Cyrulnik, 2002) conceivable? This resilience takes on significance depending on the period considered; eternal resilience leads part of the population to accept any suffering in this "lower world". We will successively see the relationship between suffering and well-being, the reduction of human suffering, a perfect obligation, then its relevance with psychoanalysis as we find concepts and economic models there.

5.1 Suffering and well-being

Since the failure of the Copenhagen summit (2010), the principle of prioritizing human suffering over economic, social, and environmental well-being has been re-discussed in the context of sustainable development. These two concepts (suffering and well-being) cannot be confused and put on the same footing. Human suffering is unbearable and cannot be compensated for by a little more well-being; it has priority.

How to think about this priority? If we give up a lexicographical principle, we must ask ourselves about the possibilities of associating possible actions on suffering and well-being.

Can we substitute well-being for suffering? The principle of the non-negotiability of human life does not permit any exceptions if the suffering is recognized as specific to the person. The optimum is then defined in relation to suffering. As a result, the human sustainability of development is very limited and has suffered multiple attacks, for example, by regulating the economy through unemployment.

5.1.1 Suffering and/or negative utility

"Classical" economic thinking favors well-being insofar as it is hedonistic and cannot accept either frustration or discomfort. Nevertheless, the economy produces, through its choices, suffering in its day-to-day activity and in its decisions (unemployment, inflation, famine, etc.).

Suffering is experienced personally even though its causes may be global (exploitation); well-being is more easily collective. Levinas (1989) reminds us that in work, in pain and in sorrow, the person perceives his/her loneliness. There is the impossibility of detaching oneself from suffering, *"it is the irremissibility of being"*. One of the tasks of the psychosociologist consists of raising the suffering from the depth of each one in order to express it and make it a collective well-being. We resist suffering as best as we can; we passively accept well-being.

Suffering is not present in economics except in the problematic of negative utility according to Karl Popper (1945). Negative utility awkwardly refers to human suffering. This more conceptual negative utility theory, ridiculed by the liberals themselves, reappeared in force after the failure of the Copenhagen environmental summit. The preservation of nature cannot be conceived without reducing human suffering. Dress human suffering through utility? Suffering does not immediately mean disutility for the person, but an attack on his/her life. Negative utility does not overlap with suffering, but simply the idea that a choice is unpleasant to us. Negative utility does not overlap with Evil, as malevolence. One can suffer without malice; this is more related to the form of altruism, to taking pleasure in the loss of utility of the Other. Human suffering is not the opposite of Good, but another dimension of life.

5.1.2 Priority to the reduction of suffering

The opposition between suffering and well-being is old. According to Kant's concept of negative magnitudes, suffering should be opposed to well-being and that the increase in suffering translates into a decrease in well-being.

This opposition is clear between contentment (Kant, 1798) and pain *"which are not only contradictory, but also contrary"*. Above all contentment is always the pain; the pain is inserted between the contentment, even if it means expressing only small inhibitions. The radical thought of the 19th century, especially anarchist, opposes the suffering of the proletarian to the well-being of the bourgeois.

Thus, according to Louise Michel (1983), *"Philosophers are bourgeois. They only consider well-being above all"*, they should *"advise on the best means to protect those who are suffering"*, but they are *"epicureans who preach the great brotherhood"*. It is the same with economists who preach justice and are only *"fierce egoists"*, *"cold despisers of humanity"*. Those who suffer are all those who are condemned to enrich the exploiters, sated, pot-bellied, and *"fat rich people who burst with indigestion"*. They will practice the general strike and thanks to the sticks in the air of the *"force which reflects"*, all will have bread. Social justice first concerns those who suffer.

When wealth increases, suffering decreases and the number of prejudices that the "creditor" can endure without suffering *"gives the measure of his wealth"* remarks Nietzsche, in *Généalogie de la morale* (1994). Thus, according to him, those who have committed the most harm to society go unpunished.

The priority given to well-being is strongly contested by the approach to suffering. From a philosophical perspective, reducing human suffering is a perfect obligation, unlike increasing well-being which is an imperfect obligation.

From an ecological point of view, strong social sustainability takes priority over strong sustainability from an environmental point of view. From a social perspective, therefore, there is a priority of reducing human suffering over increasing well-being. Well-being creates suffering, for example, lengthening the lifespan, without paying attention to the state of health. What kind of priority is this? If suffering is primary and non-negotiable, there is a lexicographic priority so that the reduction of suffering must be fully achieved before proceeding to well-being. An adjustment of this requirement can be envisaged by applying this type of priority in the form of a leximin, starting with the most vulnerable. Is this priority too high?

The economist will consider the possible combinations, between minimizing/maximizing well-being and increasing/decreasing human suffering (Table 5.1).

Suffering can increase simultaneously with the decrease or increase in well-being (cases 2 and 3); conversely, it can decrease simultaneously with the decrease or increase in well-being (cases 1 and 4).

• Case 2 (increase in suffering and decrease in well-being) corresponds well to situations of economic crisis: unemployment,
  increase in precariousness, etc. result in both a deterioration in
  living conditions (e.g. poor housing) and physical deterioration
  (difficulties in accessing healthcare) and moral (uncertainty, loss of
  self-confidence).

Table 5.1 Combinations between well-being and suffering

Suffering			
		↘	↗
Well-being	↘	1	2
	↗	4	3

- Case 3 (increase in suffering and increase in well-being) reflects the situation of industrialized economies where, due to the hedonistic illusion, access to mass consumption of material goods is facilitated (all the mechanisms of consumer credit, discount, etc.), while at the same time suffering increases (pressure at work, precarious employment conditions, over-indebtedness – in France, every day, three people commit suicide because of over-indebtedness, etc.). The excessive focus on well-being is associated with an increase in the consumption of goods, while at the same time, exploitation in the sphere of production increases suffering.
- Case 4 (decrease in suffering and increase in well-being) reflects the "ideal" situation of economic theory; no need to worry about suffering since its reduction is automatically acquired with economic development.
- Case 1 (reduction in suffering and reduction in well-being) reflects current concerns, for example, developed by supporters of "degrowth".

If rational individuals were under a *"veil of ignorance"* (Rawls, 1971), they would choose to minimize their suffering (cases 1 and 4), in the following order of priority: 4 > 1> 3 > 2.

The hedonistic illusion leads to an erroneous conception of choice since it is limited to the opposition between two alternatives, that is: 4 = 3 > 1 = 2. This assimilation makes it possible to opt for case 3 while case 1 is superior to it from a social point of view (without considering case 4 which is itself superior to case 1, but assimilated to 3). Taking suffering into account would radically change the normative judgement that is made on societies and on economic and social policies. Decisions come up against many principles: non-negotiability, universality, sovereignty, etc. Especially when it comes to choosing between human suffering and the preservation of nature. However, one can imagine compensations, between suffering and well-being, like the sacrifice of a child for ten million people. Sacrificial religions pave the way for the idea of compensation, such as the sacrifice of the son of God who came to redeem men. But apart from divine reasons, the sacrifice of a person for the salvation of others is of exemplary immorality.

One cannot, for example, sacrifice human lives for environmental improvements. The human sustainability of economic choices stops at the suffering of one person in the name of the principle of universality. Nonetheless, there is implicit bargaining in economic and environmental regulation. The principle *"leave to suffer and die"* in the relationship between rich and poor remains widely accepted.

Human suffering is personal, it calls on the sovereign person, capable of reflecting on himself/herself. It is a *"subjective impulse"* (Adorno, 1978). Modern analysis of human suffering, such as psychoanalysis, plays an important role that the economist cannot overlook. It expresses, according to Adorno, the fact of not supporting a *"loss of capacities"*; it is reflected in a primary desire to free oneself.

Suffering is then rejected by work analysts as an individual syndrome, if not complaining, the fashion being social. Suffering is a personal variable, long marginalized insofar as it does not appear socially, but personally. We can thus see the difference between social sustainability and human sustainability.

Suffering, linked to this reflection, is therefore physical and moral. It is an important factor of vulnerability and resilience capacity. Suffering promotes an "incapacity", which goes beyond the issue of capability. Suffering has negative consequences on the freedom of choice and this is very relativized. For a person in pain, freedom of choice (Sen's capability) is secondary; the person is constrained by suffering and hopes that this primary objective, to reduce the pain, will be achieved. Freedom of choice becomes perverse in the form of the choice of the means to make it disappear. A bit like the executioner who gives you the freedom to choose your means of execution. *"Evil is this inability to feel that one can cause suffering"* (Abel, 1997). The economy is the source of evil when it forgets the sacrifice.

Planning is based on the myth of sequential happiness; yet it is based on rigour and sacrifice. The trade-off between the sufferings of the partners in the economy is a major problem: how to reduce the suffering of some without increasing that of others. A solution of maximin can be put forward: maximize the decrease in suffering for some, while minimizing the consequent increase for others. Ultimately, Rawls's leximin would allow the smallest sacrifice of the wealthiest to allow the greatest advantage of the most disadvantaged.

We can thus see that there is a "hedonistic illusion" in economic teleology, by promising ultimately happiness after suffering. This illusion is much more substantial than the monetary and fiscal illusions of the current economy.

5.2 An ethics of suffering

In *The Theory of Moral Sentiments*, Adam Smith (1759) shows the importance of looking at suffering: commiseration can quickly give rise to disgust[5] in the face of strong suffering, until the absence of reaction when suffering occurs in a distant place.

However, according to Levinas, "*I am challenged by the face of every being who suffers and I feel guilty*". The suffering of the other is translated into a command to be concerned about him, but the analyst very quickly comes up against a problem of meddling with a suffering person and with non-rationalizable data: love, esteem, dignity. The non-recognition as autonomous people, even if it means being despised as individuals, is the first declared suffering of the poor. If they are suffering people, they can judge the quality of life and their dignity until they decide to reduce their suffering. Medical ethics have effected this transformation of the patient in person, the economy remains with a depersonalized individual, especially if he is poor. He is only an irresponsible individual and therefore incapable of suffering: a simple holder of well-being or, according to the current fashion, of capability. An ethics of suffering begins with the consideration of the subject "*as an end in itself and not only as a means which such or such will can use at will*".

Human suffering is experiencing a resurgence of interest in France, from the point of view of the human sciences with two major authors: Christophe Dejours and Boris Cyrulnik.

Dejours (2009) analyses suffering at work in the context of voluntary servitude; he founded psychodynamics, for example, the processes of mediating suffering in the face of injustice, accompanied by "normopathy", a pathology of submission and collaboration.

Several factors reinforce this suffering at work: in general, resignation to "economicist" justifications, tolerance of injustice but also, fear of incompetence, forced to work badly, lack of recognition, fear, and submission. There is a rationalization of the evil: thus, the economic discourse of work based on the flexibility of the labour market had its heyday by winning the Nobel Prize for Economy in 2010.

Cyrulnik (2002), in the face of fatalism, shows how the suffering resulting from abuse can be overcome and founded the concept of resilience in the social sciences. For example, an emotional vulnerability can turn into a force of affection, if you pay a price for it. While the author emphasizes the case of resilient children, resilience can be transposed to vulnerable workers.

5.2.1 An ethical imperative: not to increase suffering

The suffering of one or more people cannot be increased, on purpose, and cannot be justified! If suffering is first, there is an optimum of suffering such that a decision would not be acceptable if the suffering of one person were to increase. The tradition of the optimum goes back to Pareto's "G-spot", expressing maximum pleasure and is not justifiable in the face of suffering. Or at least compensate for an increase in suffering! Suffering is not fatal, but a threshold can be crossed, where we go from weak sustainability to strong sustainability (irreversibility, ultimate testimony). It is possible to bounce back and get out of the circle of suffering, a resilience; thus, people who suffered in their childhood are not predestined to become wicked in their turn! Suffering concerns all species and involves speciesism.

5.2.2 A heuristic of suffering: a long-term equilibrium

Compared to immediate justice (an optimum of suffering), suffering is part of a long-term equilibrium. The suffering of our present condition will be compensated in the long run by the delights of a heavenly world. Justice based on the absence of suffering is a heavenly myth; suffering is also assimilated to hellish punishment. In hell, according to the comments, the suffering is continuous, incessant, and knows no respite. The same idea is present in the Catholic religion, if not in Buddhism. This inscription of suffering in the long term is nevertheless very earthly. Suffering poses problems of time, transient ailments will have no more meaning than transient well-being (e.g. provided by drugs); if not to make the suffering even more painful in times of withdrawal.

We can distinguish several balances and therefore several justices in the long term.

- Intragenerational justice: it offers more suffering for one generation, for more happiness for another. Thus, the generation of the *baby boom* in France is paying for its comfort of life by the suffering of its children.
- Intergenerational justice: it advocates less well-being and more suffering to improve the well-being of future generations that we will not know.
- Eternal justice: the suffering endured in our life will be compensated by eternal happiness, on condition of believing in God and vice versa; woe to the rich! This belief is one of the keys to social stability. The suffering of today's world is all the more acceptable, even increased, as it will be compensated in a possible world of delights, provided you believe in it. This belief appears under multiple ethics, in the sense of adapting religions or morals to personal ends.[6] Thus, Puritanism is an adaptation of the Reformation to the needs of the English tradesmen. Ultimately, he distorts it by introducing

predestination, as a reward in heaven for the efforts made on earth. In this very general case, since resilience is post-mortem, it is permissible to undermine the principle of universal suffering. This is not one of the least interventions of religion in economic behaviour.

Taking human suffering into account calls into question the priorities of the economy; the teleology of Good is an imperfect duty, on the other hand reducing suffering is a perfect duty. We thus see the problem of the sacrifice as necessary to achieve macroeconomic regulation. The question of sacrifice arises more than ever with the debates on climate change. Should we make two billion poor people suffer and two hundred million unemployed people, to reduce the fear associated with climate change? Will the regulation of ecological disorder be achieved through human suffering? Should we liquidate thousands of unemployed to satisfy the markets and thus clear the errors of the financiers? Once again, humankind is the means to an ecological or financial end.

Restoring human suffering in economic thinking immediately poses problems of principle:

- First, the principle of priority of suffering over well-being. A standard economic calculation of opportunities combining well-being and suffering includes disgusting choices. It is not humanly sustainable. The project of development economics, whether it is based on well-being or the freedom to achieve a desired way of life (capability), is being challenged.
- Second, the moral impossibility of negotiating over the life of any person; from this point of view, the prohibition of human sacrifice is a universal principle, but one which is not respected in the current economy, locked in a hedonistic dogma. It is not easy to reconcile the universality of human suffering, the reduction of which is a priority, with respect for personal sovereignty, especially in the case of euthanasia. This poses the problem of the line between negative utility and suffering; an optimum based on this principle of non-compensation is very demanding and meets the borderline cases of the absence of envy or Pareto-unanimity.

Practically, well-being should be secondary to suffering, the most important problem being to simulate the effects of economic decisions on suffering. A classification could be made according to the precautions taken in this area by each country in its various institutions. The ideal-type of development would be the lowest level of suffering and no longer income or well-being. Different principles can be put forward.[7]

An extreme criterion of prohibiting the creation of suffering, analogous to the absence of envy, can initially be retained; then a more weakened principle admitting compensation can be established. Either, a strong principle of non-suffering, which cannot accept any decision that may increase the suffering of a person; this principle can be extended to the natural environment within the framework of a harsh ecology such as Jaïnism. Or, a weak principle of non-suffering, which condemns any action that would increase the amount of suffering, even beyond a certain limit. It is evident that extreme suffering can occur within this sum. This principle justifies, for example, the application of an employment multiplier. Peter Singer (1997) sets out a principle of equal consideration of interests and a principle of equality, conditions which call for the same precaution for different species. Finally, a principle of non-opportunism is necessary so as not to consider that a "wonderful misfortune" is deemed essential for resilience. Thus, many people believe that prior suffering is the condition for success, such as the *numerus clausus* practices that some impose on entering their activity.

5.3 Interest of psychoanalysis for the economy

Economic anthropology deals with the person and his/her physical and mental components. It appeals to psychology and psychoanalysis. It integrates the "analytical" or "clinical" concepts of the Freudian universe (relationship to the father, to the mother, and more generally subjective trauma linked to the communal unconscious). The developmental relationship can easily be posed as a "son to father" relationship or a fusional relationship to the mother in the manner of Geza Roheim (1978).

Therefore, we can understand better natural laziness, or excess productivism, exploitation or savings, etc. Paraphrasing Wittgenstein (1961), the speaker risks bringing his "private psychology", his own "clinic" into his understanding of the social phenomenon he is analysing. Freud's contribution to anthropology and therefore to economics remains to be clarified. If the person is built with a superego, there is "a fight of the individual against society" where the ideals and the ethical requirements exceed the capacities of the person. This collective superego that Freud evokes in *Le malaise dans la culture* implies, in human behaviour and particularly in economic acts, the tension of guilt, anxiety, aggressiveness, and more generally disturbances.

Economic anthropology integrates Freud's borrowings from economic theory. Conversely, economists (Kolm in particular) question the schizophrenia of economic agents, and their disturbances in the trade-off between egoism and altruism.

We have already underlined behaviour in relation to time, which is a function of both selfish disturbances and community disturbances.

A similar lag exists for variables when they are personal and not individual. Indeed, they are interpreted in terms of responsibility and community pressure. The salary becomes the lever of redistribution and community protection. A reduction in salary, interpreted in relation to the consequent community disturbances, will entail a more than proportional reduction in the official work provided. Conversely, a salary increase can be refused if it causes a more than proportional increase in community pressure. We can thus speak of community resilience, if not of a resilient community.

Psychoanalysis is condemned in the name of the morality of economists, namely hedonism. If economists have incorporated advances in the theory of justice, they pretend nothing has happened in psychiatry. Can they stick to Edgeworth's *Mathematical Psychics* (1881) and his blunt talk about pleasure, which he says is more important for men than for women? Can pleasure and desire be treated by economic analysis? In fact, much of economic theory deals with pleasure. Several authors, for example, Brentano (1874), establish a mathematical relationship between physical stimuli and sensations, a kind of "psychophysics". As arousal increases geometrically, sensation increases arithmetically. There is, thus, a subjective assessment of value which would no longer be objective. Here we find one of the foundations of the theory of action. At the same time, this theory of attenuation of pleasure makes people smile, as does Pareto's "hill of pleasure".

Wilfredo Pareto is, according to Nicolaï (1974), one of the rare socioeconomists to integrate elements of Freudianism,[8] but poses the problem of optimality in obscure terms: "*We have, above this, a kind of hill on which a point moves, which represents the state of the person considered. The higher the point, the more well-being the person has. The top of the hill is at G*".

Keynes, who calls himself "pre-Freudian"[9] celebrates in Freud

> the scientific imagination which can give shape to an abundance of innovative ideas, to shattering openings, to working hypotheses which are sufficiently established in intuition and in common experience to merit the most patient and impartial examination, and which contains, in all probability, both theories which will have to be abandoned or

reworked until they no longer exist, but also theories of immense and permanent significance.

(Bormans, 2002)

Freud's theories are to be *"taken seriously"*, *"the attraction they will exert on our own intuitions, insofar as they contain something new and true about the way human psychology works"* (ibid.). Freud is *"one of the most disturbing and innovative geniuses of our time, which is to say a kind of devil"* (ibid.)

Keynes gives a very critical interpretation of the love of money, in other words, the pecuniary motivation is *"one of those half-criminal and half-pathological inclinations which one shudderingly entrusts to specialists in mental disease"*.

> *The love of money as an object of possession, which must be distinguished from the love of money as a means of procuring the pleasures and realities of life, will be recognized for what it is: a rather repugnant morbid state.*

(Keynes, 1936)

However, Keynes botches the subject, going to Descartes to find the evocation of "animal spirits". These characterize irrational behaviour, without going deeper into the analysis of neuroses arising from the economic context.

5.4 Economic concepts and models

The reading of Freud's work is carried out from an economic perspective by Ricoeur in *Le conflit des interprétations. Essais d'herméneutique* (2013). There are many references to be found there, from an economic model of compensation to the concepts of investment and work, and a problem of balance.

5.4.1 A principle of compensation

Paul Ricoeur (2013) interprets Freud's *"economic model of the phenomenon of culture"* as "the *economic interpretation which dominates all Freudian considerations on culture*". Culture is made up of coercion and renunciation. These instinctual sacrifices must be compensated. What can be the nature of this compensation which, in economics, aims to correct the optimum damage or externalities? The solution to the conflict is highly codified in the form of bargaining versus taxation. In

Freud's theory, compensation is provided by a primordial hostility of man to man. Here come the death drive and the need to punish. The death drive does not translate into acting out, but through a feeling of guilt.

In "Deuil et mélancolie" (2010), Freud questions the economic means for resolving mourning. For example, the reward could be one of these ways. How to reduce the expenses of refoulement? The work of mourning involves a devaluation of the Ego with a devastating death drive that the Superego tries to curb. Mourning involves a profusion of energy, a counter-investment in the face of investing in the search for the lost being.

5.4.2 An intrapersonal equilibrium

According to Nicolaï (1999), economics and psychoanalysis have in common a principle of pleasure and a principle of reality.

The pleasure principle translates into economy by the search for maximum satisfaction, and in psychoanalysis by the maximum realization of the drives.

The principle of reality is expressed in economics by budgetary constraints, and in psychoanalysis by the desire for repression.

There is an intrapersonal balance, unique to each person. Excessive satisfaction in economics can correspond to a psychological deficit. This last case will be a factor of suffering, especially through dreams, mistakes, phobias, melancholia, etc. Freud analyses these imbalances and especially their consequences on people: schizophrenia, paranoia, etc.

Utility is thus counterbalanced by suffering. Bentham's pleasures and pains have only been studied at the level of pleasures; this incompleteness of economic analysis is resolved by taking suffering into account.

This relationship between pleasure and suffering, or even between pain and satisfaction can be analysed using traditional economic tools (indifference curves, marginal rate of substitution, optimum, etc.).

There are therefore two types of economicity, one at the level of the market, the other at the level of the person, two types which have never been able to be associated.

5.4.3 Extensions

Masochism is treated as an economic problem; it represents an exception to the general rule of seeking pleasure, as a pleasure experienced in suffering, hence resignation in the face of injustice. According to

Dejours (2009), society is made up of "normopaths" resigned to the aggressive impulses of authority.

The aggressive drive is a major economic agent for Nicolaï (1999), one of the few economists to study the integration of the Ego into society. This integration through aggression makes it possible to understand the social revenges inherent in the rise of power; or the will to kill the father, like the Karamazov brothers.

Sexual perversions in the search for power are not innocent and can change the political situation of a country, if not the economic choices of a continent. Ultimately, microeconomic calculation is constrained by the budget, intrapersonal calculation by the culture of frustration. The need is constrained in fact, by the budget but also by saturation; there is a double constraint in which community frustration (e.g. totems and taboos) plays a determining role. Resilience consists of removing the cultural constraint as much as possible to focus on the budget constraint.

Let us assume a classic representation of the relation between consumption and income, by specifying an incompressible consumption of the person (responsible at the intra and intergenerational level).

In a flexible economy, consumption is rigid with respect to income due to intra and intergenerational transfers, up to the point where income ensures minimum fulfilment of obligations. However, the person can modify his/her transfer constraint by substituting time for income, either by deferring obligations over time, or by modifying the time allocation within the period. In this case, the person will consume more. Nevertheless, the person is susceptible to several types of constraints; three types of constraints come into play: personal, community, budgetary.

The constraints play in a given direction: first cultural (degree of frustration), then community (taboos, prohibitions, collective rules), and finally budgetary (is my income sufficient?).

Freudian calculus is more complex than utilitarian calculus.[10] It brings into play three actors: the Ego, the Id, and the Superego; three actors whose balance of power depends on the initial impulses (of two types, Eros and Thanatos) which relate to pleasure. The initial drive can come from the oedipal trauma (in the boy: sexual desire of the mother, fear of castration, and desire to kill the father/rival).

The main epistemological problem arises from the unconscious part of this calculation and the difficulty of observation, with all the risks of self-projection and transference.

The neutrality of utilitarian calculation is far from being guaranteed by an impartial spectator or any kind of equiprobability (Harsanyi, 1995). The result is that the pleasure principle, *"guardian of life"* according to Freud, can be thwarted and that suffering can be a warning of these dysfunctions; suffering that is integrated into the intrapersonal calculation and absent from the sole calculation of well-being. These sufferings are not mere annoyances and proceed from serious neurosis until the *"ultimate witness"*. We can see the interest of this pathology in the implementation of a precautionary principle in the face of economic decisions.

Culture and budget are thus linked, in particular, psychological dispositions and monetary availability at the level of constraints; constraints that weigh on pleasure, desire, impulses, and needs. Capability, freedom of choice, depends on cultural constraint like the other elements, especially if it is interpreted as a sexual drive, hence the possibility of incapability. Should we liberate this capability, this potential drive, as proposed by Wilhelm Reich (1946) and vitalism? Or manage vital energy like an entrepreneur manages his capital? Freedom is conceived in cultural development *"which makes it subject to restrictions, and justice demands that no one be spared these restrictions"* (Freud, 1930). Freedom is appreciated in the balance of power between community power and individual power; a relationship that is the basis of cultural development. The small community (caste, layer of population, tribe) behaves like a violent individual and this violence spreads to other masses. The community is at the base of the *"malaise in the culture"*.

Conclusion

Personal suffering in society is a dimension hardly accepted in economics in the name of hedonism, illustrated, for example, by Pareto's *"hill of pleasure"*.

And yet the economic calculation is incomplete within this framework and it is time to integrate into it other constitutive elements of the person (Ego, Id, Superego) of his/her choices (desires, frustrations, impulses, traumas), without forgetting the fear of community constraints, highlighted by Freud.

Human suffering is unrecognized in economic theory; it concerns the person and is an extension of his/her vulnerability. Nonetheless, it appears in the form of negative utility with Karl Popper, but it is mostly the pain that points to a specific point in the person. Suffering can cover an increase in well-being, as shown by the Easterlin paradox (1974). The reduction of suffering is a perfect obligation, a priority over well-being. There are several levels of suffering depending on whether it can be compensated or not. From an ethical point of view, it is not permissible to increase a person's suffering. This calls into question the suffering that precedes a reward, illustrated, for example, by structural adjustment plans, or redundancies, which are said to be necessary for the creation of jobs. It is paradoxical that unemployment is required in order to increase employment.

Finally, this suffering concerns the mind, whose pathologies, such as burnout, are being recognized little by little and represent the majority of illnesses at work, but also in family life and more generally in society, for example: by a lack of recognition. Psychoanalysis uses many tools of economic analysis; thus, Freud perceives the pleasure principle as an economic principle.

Notes

1 This is about the suffering (physical and moral pain) produced by the economy, not suffering in general.
2 According to Ch. Dejours (1993): "*To hold resignation for a happy resolution of the castration complex and for a recognition of the real, as some analysts think, amounts, in fact, to validating the cleavage between the ego and the ideal of the me*".
3 "*I even wonder how the main feature of our relationship with death [suffering] has escaped the attention of philosophers*", Levinas (1989).
4 The desire for appropriation, anger, and ignorance are "*the three poisons*" of the mind according to the Buddha and represent the main causes of suffering.
5 Rousseau evoked as early as 1755: "*The innate reluctance to see one's fellow man suffer*"; such a sentiment being developed in Adam Smith's *Theory of Moral Sentiments*.
6 Spirit of capitalism and religious ethics are intimately linked. Max Weber's thesis reminds us that in the context of the ideological revolution of the 17th century, the spirit of capitalism adapts the Protestant religion to its practical ends, in the form of Puritanism. This ethos is made up of individualism, utilitarianism, hedonism, liberalism, and the values of the 17th century English revolution. Capitalism finds its rationality in the Puritan ethics on the occasion of this revolution.
7 Different from the principles enacted by Derek Parfit (1984): *Limited Suffering Principle, Total Suffering Principle*.
8 This contribution is limited by the fact that Pareto died in 1923, certain major works of Freud being published after this date, in particular the *Malaise dans la culture* in 1930, object of the wrath of Hayek.
9 This relationship is particularly well dealt with by Dostaler and Maris (2010).
10 Maximizing the expected utility of a decision, made up of opinions and judgements about the consequences of the decision, is a central concept of

rationality (Suppes, 1966), including economics. This use of utility, like the concept as use value, is it functional or does it proceed from Benthamite utilitarianism?

References

Abel, O., 1997, "Justice et Mal", in A. Garapon, D. Salas (eds) *La justice et le mal*, Paris: Odile Jacob, 113–144.

Adorno, T., 1978, *Dialectique négative*, Paris: Payot.

Behar, R., 1997, "De la souffrance de l'individu à la souffrance de la société", *Communication*, Paris: Académie des Sciences Morales et Politiques.

Bormans, C., 2002, *Keynes et Freud. De la "vision" à la "révolution" keynésienne: l'hypothèse Freud*, www.psychanaliste.paris.com/Keynes-et-Freud.html

Brentano, F., 2008, *Psychologie du point de vue empirique* (1874), Paris: Librairie Philosophique Vrin.

Cyrulnik, B., 2002, *Un merveilleux malheur*, Paris: Odile Jacob.

Dejours, C., 1993, *Travail: usure mentale. De la psychopathologie à la psychodynamique du travail*, Paris: Bayard.

Dejours, C., 2009, *Souffrance en France, la banalisation de l'injustice sociale*, Paris: Editions du Seuil.

Dostaler, G., Maris, B., 2010, *Capitalisme et pulsion de mort*, Paris: Pluriel.

Easterlin, R., 1974, "Does Economic Growth Improve the Human Lot? Some Empirical Evidence", in David, P. and Reder, M.W. (eds) *Nations and Households in Economic Growth: Essays in Honor of Moses Abramovitz*, New York and London, Academic Press Inc. 89–125.

Edgeworth, Y.E., 1881, *Mathematical Psychics*, London: C. Keagan.

Freud, S., 2010, "Deuil et mélancolie", *Metapsychologie* (1915), Paris: PUF, Quadrige.

Freud, S., 2015, *Le malaise dans la culture* (1930), Paris: PUF, Quadrige.

Harsanyi, J.C., 1955, "Cardinal Welfare, Individual Ethics and Intercomparison of Utility", *Journal of Political Economy*, 63: 309–321.

Kant, E., 1993, *Anthropologie du point de vue pragmatique* (1798), Paris: GF-Flammarion.

Keynes, J.M., 1936, *The General Theory of Employment, Interest, and Money*, Cambridge University Press, for the Royal Economic Society Cambridge University Press.

Levinas, E., 1989, *Le temps et l'autre*, Paris: Quadrige-PUF.

Michel, L., 1983, *Souvenirs et aventures de ma vie*, Paris: Maspero, réédition des *Mémoires*.

Nicolaï, A., 1974, "Anthropologie des économistes", *Revue Economique*, 4: 578–610.

Nicolaï, A., 1999, *Comportement économique et structures sociales* (1960), Paris: L'Harmattan, Economie et Innovation, Série Krisis.

Nietzsche, F., 1994, *Généalogie de la Morale*, Paris: Essais-Folio.

Parfit, D., 1984, *Reasons and Persons*, Oxford: Clarendon Press.

Popper, K.R., 1945, *The Open Society and Its Ennemies*, Princeton: Princeton U. Press.

Rawls, J., 1971, *A Theory of Justice*, The Belknap Press, Harvard University.

Reich, W., 1946, *La psychologie de masse du fascisme*, Paris: Payot.

Ricoeur, P., 2013, *Le conflit des interprétations. Essais d'herméneutique*, Paris: Editions du Seuil, Points-Essais.

Roheim, G., 1978, *Psychanalyse et anthropologie: culture, personnalité, inconscient*, Paris: Gallimard.

Rousseau, J.J., 1992, "Discours sur l'économie politique", *Ecrits politiques* (1755), Paris: Livre de Poche.

Singer, P., 1997, *Questions d'éthique pratique*, Paris: Bayard.

Smith, A., 1999, *Théorie des sentiments moraux* (1759), Paris: PUF, Quadrige.

Suppes, P, 1966, "Some Models of Grading Principles", *Synthèse*, 16: 184–306.

Weber, M., 1992, *Essais sur la théorie de la science*, Paris: Agora.

Wittgenstein, L., 1961, *Tractacus logico-philosophicus*, Paris: Gallimard.

Conclusion

Since it was mentioned, economic anthropology has been a place of confrontation between anthropologists and economists.

Anthropology and economics seem irreconcilable, as do positivism and formalism. Economic anthropology is thus an oxymoron, bringing together everything and its opposite. However, these two approaches complement each other: in particular, the economy needs to go beyond the stage of *homo oeconomicus* to be opened to the responsible person.

This ability to impute a responsibility, to self-constrain, ontologically grounds the person, as an *a priori* constraint that diverges from consequential responsibility, the only conception of its imputation. Economic anthropology shows the priority of community computing, with its constraints, over the market. It completes several areas neglected by economists: vulnerability, suffering, feelings, violence, etc. It analyses human behaviour by integrating psychoanalysis.

Conversely, economic theory makes it possible to enrich anthropology through its methods and models.

Nevertheless, economic anthropology goes beyond a simple observation by becoming normative through the "eminent" place given to the *a priori* vulnerable and suffering person. Ultimately, economic anthropology refocuses economics on the person and his/her life experiences. This method includes a social fact without immediately involving abstract theory and its models. These collective representations modify the usual explanation of the main markets, employment, goods, services, finance.

The fact of focusing on humankind, by re-situating him/her as a total person, implies lifting the taboo of psychoanalysis in economics. Economics and sexuality are inseparable, as are substantivism and formalism, in the development of a personal dimension. Economic anthropology is positive in nature, it is based on fieldwork data, but by recognizing the person it takes on a normative value. The person is

DOI: 10.4324/9781003386742-7

universal, s/he is worthy of respect when s/he satisfies his/her rights and obligations.

In summary, the contributions of economic anthropology are as follows, in relation to the subject, the values, the necessary disciplines.

The person, because of responsibility, is susceptible to fragility and suffering. The person completes the identity if not the supposed irrationality of individuals. S/he has a capacity structure, to speak, to do, to impute, to narrate. The responsibility that is attributed to the person can be disproportionate and weaken him/her.

The person is immersed in a world of obligations and rights, s/he is "being there". The person can rationalize his/her responsibility, but within the limits set by his/her background; s/he must remain reasonable, depending on the others.

The person is in a plurivalent relationship with others. His/her altruism, his/her social capital, his/her usefulness, his/her responsibility can be positive, neutral, negative. Conversely, s/he can be rejected by those around him/her while granting them positive altruism. Far from hedonism and well-being, s/he primarily encounters fragility and suffering. Suffering is no longer just physical; it is increasingly moral, dialectically linked to the type of production. This suffering is a matter of psychiatry. Factors come into play: consideration of the field, analysis of mentalities.

The person becomes a norm and deserves protection, as a subject of a human economy. This is the function of resilience.

The literature on resilience begins in the 1950s on the protective factors of children facing risk and allowing them to escape, through a mechanism called "resilience" (Tisseron, 2007). The risk of suffering in the economy, experienced by vulnerable people, must therefore be counterbalanced by a precautionary principle and mechanisms, both human and social. The precautionary principle is not limited to assessing risks. It comes up against the diversity of risks and uncertainties, various types of sustainability,[1] and a hierarchy of problems. Numerous analyses can reinforce precaution: decision trees, value trees, multicriteria analyses, sensitivity analyses, scenario analyses.

The principle of human and social precaution is active: research must be speeded up on uncertainties, the possible damages and solutions must be assessed using comparative scenarios. It thus opens the way to the responsibility of experts and institutions in the face of uncertainty about the social environment itself and its reactions to shocks. For example, we know that the reaction capacities of poor people are fragile: interwoven allocations of time, *inter vivos* transfers, and depend on the type of altruism practiced. However, these relationships between the policies of experts and the destruction of fragile social environments are not currently known. This principle implies, that if the studies conclude that social environments are fragile, the expert engages his penal responsibility in the event that he has significant decision-making power. It is necessary to evaluate the imputations, the shares of responsibility *a priori*. This assessment is a difficult step. It encounters hierarchy problems and decision chains (examples of the grocer who closes because of our preferences for the mini-market, of the executive who works so well that his collaborator becomes useless). What are the indicators of vulnerability or resilience? Direct or indirect responsibility? Weak or strong sustainability? Passive or active crime?

The charges must be specified *a priori*: what is the scale of the damage? The *a priori* responsibility is determined by the ethics of discussion. The ethics of discussion are based on the "democratic perspective", that is, on knowledge and judgment, the perspective of "complexity". Contingent valuation is based on the local community and its ability to reveal value and willingness to charge. This is to collect as much qualitative data as possible through a small group survey with a moderator on responsibilities, trying to find consensus. There is at this level a risk of "statistical epistemology": knowledge then depends on the conduct of the survey and its independence vis-à-vis value judgements and the "background" of the statistician. In particular, the classification by rank allows hazardous results according to the established thresholds.

In his lectures, Lévi-Strauss recalls that anthropology must respond to the problems of the modern world. His studies on kinship, for example, can be compared to the economic analysis of the family carried out by economists such as Robert Barro or Gary Becker.

Barro's theorem (1974) assumes that the old protect the young "step by step" and that this invalidates macroeconomic policies. The theorem is very simplistic and asks for details on family relations, for example, by replacing the old by the maternal uncles in an avuncular system. The anthropological question, namely the question of the subject in economics, remains unaddressed, despite the importance given to the individual in microeconomics and, since 1990, to the person supporting capabilities in human development.

This book shows how economic anthropology complements individualism and hedonism, the two pillars of choice ethics according to Arrow.

Ultimately, economic anthropology favours a return to the person in economics. This return to the subject is even more important because reasoning by aggregates or by social class has shown its limits, as has the hedonistic principle. The economy is a place not only of happiness, but also of unhappiness; unhappiness being the consequences of bad policies. More generally, political economy is at the service of the person and not the person at the service of the aggregates. The aggregates do not suffer!

Note

1 In the case of weak sustainability, resilience is possible; on the other hand, strong sustainability cannot give rise to resilience. In the latter case, the deaths, for example, are irreversible.

References

Barro, R., 1974, "Are Government Bonds Net Wealth?", *Journal of Political Economy*, 82, 6: 1095–1117.

Tisseron, S., 2007, *La résilience*, Paris: PUF, Que sais-je.

Glossary

Agency

In the social and human sciences, this expression emphasizes the ability to act in connection with others towards a common end.

Agent

The concept of agent broadens and goes beyond that of individual. S/he is someone who is autonomous, capable of defining his/her own choices and carrying them out rationally, by allocating resources to them for a given purpose. Unlike the individual, this purpose goes beyond his/her sole interest. Therefore, s/he can be attributed a responsibility, because s/he has a capacity for action oriented towards a chosen end. We will speak of an economic agent when the finality is economic.

Altruism

Refers to the fact of being "interested" in the Other (Levinas).

Contemporary economics departs from the original sociological interpretation by retaining only a benevolent (positive) conception of altruism in the form of compassion and commitment. This translates into economics by integrating the utility of the Other into the utility function of an individual (my satisfaction increases when the satisfaction of the other increases). Thus, it rejects any possibility of malevolent (negative) altruism: my satisfaction increases when the satisfaction of the other decreases.

Anthropology

Deals with the question *"What is a humankind?"*. It is expressed in different forms.

Cultural anthropology

First form of anthropology which studied the characteristics of so-called primitive societies. Nowadays, this discipline seeks to identify the cultural invariants of humanity.

Economic anthropology

Examines the links between economic phenomena, production, consumption, trade, and the universal human subject, namely the person.

Physical anthropology

Examines the physical diversity of humanity and its consequences in terms of economic, health, social, performance, etc.

Social anthropology

Examines the diversity of societies in their specific characteristics, modes of production and reproduction, social interactions and exchanges.

Autonomy

The autonomy of an agent implies, according to Amartya Sen, that s/he has the ability to rationally define his/her choices. However, s/he is not considered independent because s/he can be part of a social network and make choices that commit himself/herself morally.

This view of autonomy is characteristic of the agent and therefore differs from that of the individual.

Capability

Linked to the work of Amartya Sen, this neologism designates the freedom to rationally choose the desired way of life between different alternatives.

This term describes the set of achievements that an agent is able, and would be able, to make or be, faced with a set of opportunities.

Capability includes a dimension of achievement, effective and observable, and a potential dimension of achievement, in front of possible alternatives. The set of "accomplished functionings" traces what a person is currently capable of doing and being, and the set of "freedoms of choice" traces what s/he could do or be, in a different context facing better opportunities.

Promoting the capabilities of people, through functionings and freedoms, is the goal of human development.

Capacities

Concern the founding capacities characterizing the person, namely speaking, writing, narrating, and assuming responsibility (Ricoeur, 2004).

Dignity

Translates the ability to fulfil one's rights and duties (Kant). The fight against poverty and social exclusion, and more broadly development, must include as a primary objective the restoration of the dignity of persons.

Envy

Expresses the fact of preferring the endowment of the Other to his own. A long theoretical tradition equates the absence of envy with justice. The idea can be put forward that in a world of envy (if there is no justice), measures are taken in order to equalize either the well-being of individuals, or their resources. Such an idea is rejected by Nozick (1974) for whom economic equality cannot suppress envy.

Envy isn't all negative and malicious. It can indeed be negative by aiming to reduce the endowment of the Other; it can also be positive by creating emulation (Schoeck, 1995).

Ethics

Ethics expresses the reflexive dynamic that relates to moral choices, sometimes observed (positive ethics), sometimes discussed to question their consistency in order to extract relevant moral standards (normative ethics).

The practice differentiates between ethics and moral despite the fact that, etymologically common, they designate the same object, namely mores. The difference between ethics and moral is deepened by Paul Ricoeur (1990), relying on Aristotle and Kant, between "*what is considered good*" or "*teleological aim*" and "*what is imposed as obligatory*".

Ethics of responsibility

Responsibility founds the person. It also founds the economy. Each person is responsible for his/her own survival and that of others; s/he must work to meet his/her obligations.

Fallibility

This concept, put forward by Paul Ricoeur (1960), refers to the ability to make mistakes following disproportionate obligations, particularly from the point of view of responsibility.

Freedom

According to Voltaire, it is about *"the freedom to do what I want"* or the absence of constraints.

Sen adopts a particular form of freedom: freedom of choice or capability.

The freedom to suppress freedom (Arendt, 1958) or even the desire for fascism (Fromm, 1941) emphasizes the relativity of freedom.

Inner freedom

A person can consent, by voluntary self-restraint, to obligations that limit his/her freedom; this for the sake of responsibility (Rousseau, Kant).

Negative freedom

Emphasizes obstacles to freedom and traces the fact of being able to be free to make choices only in a world of constraints determined by others or by institutions. The problem comes from the fact that we do not distinguish, among these constraints, those which are suffered from those which we can impose on ourselves when we feel responsible *a priori* (*ex ante*) for a certain number of social obligations.

Positive freedom

Represents all that a person can effectively accomplish, regardless of constraints imposed by others, or by institutions. It expresses the capacity to make his/her own choices and therefore ignores obligations, even voluntarily accepted.

Good (Sovereign Good)

Aristotle, at the beginning of *Ethique à Nicomaque*, reminds us that we cannot choose one thing indefinitely in view of another. There is an ultimate end, or Sovereign Good, towards which our action must tend. The theory of Good is inseparable from a universal conception of the authority of free men over their environment.

Goulet, Denis (1931–2006)

He is considered a pioneer in development ethics with the publication of his article "Pour une éthique moderne du développement" in the journal *Développement et civilisation* (1960). He combines a phenomenological approach for the analysis of situations, and a field approach when designing public actions and policies.

Happiness

"Activity in accordance with Virtue" according to Aristotle.

Happiness consists of living according to our personality so that we can enjoy life and the world with the richest possible sensitivity.

Bentham reminds us that *"one man's happiness will never be another man's happiness"*, that their addition can only be postulated because there is a problem of common measure.

Identity

Identity is made up of the characteristics of the person: social class, gender, profession, sport, race, religion, etc. The fact that the agents present themselves under various identities opens up tolerance towards others. The recognition of the different capabilities and freedoms around these identities promotes democracy. Identity is a source of commitment and responsibility; it can also be a source of conflict.

Individual

This is the individual of microeconomics, whose autonomy expresses independence from others, and whose rationality consists in maximizing his/her interest or satisfaction.

Jonas, Hans (1903–1993)

German historian and philosopher, he is considered the philosopher of sustainable development. His main work, *Le principe responsabilité: une éthique pour la civilisation technologique* (1979), denounces not only attacks on the environment, but also the automation of work, the control of behaviour, and forms of domination. The person endowed with an infinite responsibility towards future generations is placed at the heart of his analysis.

He states: *"Act in such a way that the effects of your action are compatible with the permanence of an authentically human life on earth"*.

Levinas, Emmanuel (1906–1995)

French philosopher known for his ethics of the face; the face is the expression of the Other. The responsibility towards the Other is infinite and founds the person. This erasure of the individual in favour of the person is dealt with in *Totalité et infini* (1961) or in *Humanisme de l'autre homme* (1972).

Levinas proposes a philosophy of the relationship with the Other at a given moment of time. Money facilitates this relationship and avoids justice based on revenge and forgiveness.

Malevolence

Consists of wanting evil for others. Malevolence is materialized in economics by the idea of negative altruism: my utility increases when the utility of the other decreases. In fact, in economics, it is rarely mentioned given the hedonism inherent in this discipline.

Moral

Concerns what is imposed as obligatory by means of norms resulting from reflections on positive ethics and normative ethics. These norms, which aim to guide people's moral choices, are characterized by their universality and their constraints. Moral opposes Good to Evil.

Obligations

In any society, faced with rights, there are obligations and a socially constructed balance between rights and obligations.

Kant opposes the so-called imperfect obligations (towards others), and the so-called perfect obligations (towards oneself).

Halévy (1901) considers that utilitarianism rejects obligation as a primary notion; the obligation is only conceivable in the case of a service rendered.

The capability approach emphasizes effective rights and corresponding freedoms, with a tendency to forget obligations that often take priority and raise a question of *ex ante* responsibility. Sen, taking up the distinction of Kant, favours "perfect" obligations and *ex post* responsibility.

Optimum

In its most systematic version, intuitively the simplest, it designates *"an achievable state over which no other achievable state is preferred"*

(Debreu, 1966); in other words, a situation preferred over any other. We deduce that if we want to do better for some agents, others will be less satisfied.

Poverty optimum

In a situation of extreme poverty, people may nevertheless consider that, for them, this state is preferable to any other; hence the importance of taking into account the feelings of poor populations.

Other (The)

The Other as *"the face of the Other"* (Levinas) imposes himself/herself on me, s/he makes me responsible.

Economic theory struggles to take the Other into account since s/he is, by nature, specific.

If Levinas's approach delimits the Other in the present (the face of the Other), that of Jonas tries to take him/herself into account in the future (the generations to come, which we will not know).

Pareto-unanimity

All individuals, for all possible choices, have the same preference.

It is a condition on the aggregation of choices that is paradoxical: irreconcilable with freedom, it can become the basis of totalitarianism. Therefore the optimum can be dictatorial.

Person

Entity built beyond the individual by his/her capacities, in particular to self-constrain. This concept is part of a society of rights and obligations, unlike the individual of the society of nature.

The concept of person broadens and goes beyond the concept of economic agent. It is the positive observation of ethical choices that imposes the introduction of the concept of person. In fact, we observe that only the person is capable of imputing to himself/herself, by commitment or by going beyond, an *ex ante* responsibility towards others or the environment. This responsibility can lead him/her to voluntarily accept a reduction in his/her freedom.

Sen uses this term more and more frequently in his writings. However, he does not give a precise anthropological definition; which would allow him to be assigned the corresponding level of responsibility.

Phenomenology

School of philosophical thought that sets out to describe economic and social phenomena as they appear in their entirety. This leads to taking into account social interactions, perceptions, motivations, and social representations, as well as the intentionality of people. This is an essential approach for studying heterogeneous and rapidly changing societies.

Amartya Sen's approach is outside this school of thought, even if some of his reflections on existence, disability, sustainable development, or identity may open a reflection in this direction.

Economic phenomenology

Reconstruction of economic reasoning on the basis, not of the individual, but of the person considered positively, and not normatively as an ideal in the manner of Emmanuel Mounier. Immersed in a world of rights and obligations, the person is first of all responsible and endowed with capacities in the sense of Paul Ricoeur. In addition, the person is vulnerable, fragile, and must be considered with caution. S/he deserves protection as much as nature, against the suffering resulting from other people; reducing suffering takes priority over increasing well-being.

Resilience

Metaphor which designates the capacity of a (natural) system or of (human) agents to absorb without rupture, then to overcome, the consequences of a shock (expected or unexpected, endogenous or exogenous), recovering after the corresponding crisis their integrity and their main functions.

Responsibility

In the legal sense, it is a question of imputing an act to a person in order to envisage a compensation or a sanction, which refers to the term responsibility in the sense of accountability.

In the philosophical sense, it is about reflecting on the consequences of one's actions (responsiveness). In this sense, the concept relates to the commitment of the person to do an action, for oneself or for others.

Ex ante *responsibility*

Results from the presence of *a priori* obligations which may have the effect of reducing the freedom of action.

Also called *"prospective responsibility"*, it corresponds to feeling responsible for others. This responsibility imposes self-constraint on one's own freedom in order to fulfil obligations that are considered to a priority.

Ex post *responsibility*

Results from the *a posteriori* consequences of the actions carried out, it is therefore directly linked to the freedom to act. Also called *"retrospective responsibility"*, it corresponds to the fact of answering to others for one's errors.

Responsibility, principle

Title of the best-known work by Hans Jonas for whom the development of science and technology constitutes a threat to nature and humanity; not only for the present generation, but also in the very long term for future generations, which we will not know. To protect nature and humanity in the face of irreversible risks, Jonas introduces a categorical principle, responsibility. It states a "duty to be" so that humanity is and subsists, which obliges us to think of a new moral rule which allows the permanence of an *"authentically human life on earth"*.

Ricoeur, Paul (1913–2005)

French philosopher whose originality is to analyse the capacity for action (agency) of the person. By assuming responsibilities, the person generates a disproportion of his/her obligations vis-à-vis himself/herself and others; hence his/her fallibility, vulnerability, and fragility.

He proposes a distinction between ethics (what is good) and moral (what is required as compulsory). At the centre of his thought, the *"ethical aim"* is defined as *"Aim for a good life with and for others in just institutions"*.

Rights

Characterize the situation of the person in relation to his/her social environment, and above all determine his/her *ex ante* responsibility. Every society evolves through a subtle balance between rights and obligations; rights are often not effective until obligations have been fulfilled.

Having rights does not automatically imply their transformation into capabilities. Moreover, in order to meet the obligations, it is often necessary to give up certain freedoms, which suggests a "responsibility capability" of which Sen does not speak.

Sen, Amartya (1933–)

Indian economist and philosopher, specialist in social choice theory, but also in poverty and development issues, he received the Bank of Sweden Prize in Economic Sciences in memory of Alfred Nobel, the Nobel Prize for Economy, in 1998 for *"his contribution to the welfare economy"*.

He places freedom at the heart of his development analysis. This results in the concept of capability, which designates the freedom to choose one's way of life. *"The set of capabilities thus expresses the real freedom a person has to choose between the different lives s/he can lead"* (Sen, 1993).

Spectrum

Representation of the scale of values that certain ethical concepts can take. For example, altruism, as the relationship between my utility and that of the other, is not necessarily positive, but can be negative or neutral.

Subject

A philosophical concept which covers, in a generic way, all the definitions relating to the individual, the agent and the person, starting from the distinction between subject and object.

Suffering

Suffering (different from pain) corresponds to the physical and moral degradations of the person.

This notion has been abandoned by economists (except in particular analyses, such as suffering at work), in favour of well-being and happiness in the name of the belief that the increase in well-being and happiness would automatically lessen the suffering.

For Ricoeur, suffering is linked to a deprivation of capacities. Suffering promotes an "incapacity" which has negative consequences on the freedom of choice. For a person who suffers, the freedom of choice (the capability of Sen) is secondary. Thus, suffering is an important factor of vulnerability.

Restoring suffering in economics raises two main issues:

- The principle of priority of suffering over well-being. The reduction of suffering is a perfect obligation, the increase of well-being, an imperfect obligation.

- The principle of the moral impossibility of negotiating on the life of any person. The human sustainability of economic, environmental, and social choices stops at the suffering of a single person.

Transfers

In development economics, this term usually designates the remittances sent by migrants to their families in the country of origin (individual transfers) or to their village committees to contribute to various collective projects (collective transfers).

But transfers can exist before any international migration; they are imposed on every individual as a set of rights and obligations resulting from his/her social status, rank in the family (eldest), etc.

It is possible to distinguish transfers according to their form: in money, in kind (shipments of food products, medicines, etc.), in labour (at harvest time), in time (funerals, visits). The different forms of transfers are substitutable.

Utilitarianism

Originally, utilitarianism is a moral made up of rules of behaviour. Then it becomes a mode of evaluation of objects by economics and tends to be reduced in the theory of well-being to the Pareto optimum.

Virtue

Designates a set of qualities of the person to do Good and contributing to a "good life"; these are, in particular, the four cardinal virtues: wisdom, temperance, courage, and justice.

Vulnerability

Expresses the probability, for an agent, of losing well-being following, for example, job loss, inflation, natural disaster, etc. Strengthening certain capabilities, combining or substituting others, can contribute to increasing the resilience capacity of the most vulnerable agents, who are also often the poorest, faced with such situations.

References

Arendt, H., 1958, *Condition de l'homme moderne*, Paris: Agora.
Aristote, 1990, *Ethique à Nicomaque*, Paris: Librairie Philosophique Vrin.

Debreu, G., 1966, *La théorie de la valeur*, Paris: Dunod.

Fromm, E., 1941, *Escape from Freedom*, New York: Editions Rinehart and Winston.

Halévy, E., 1901, *La formation du radicalisme philosophique* (3 vol.), Paris: Félix Alcan, 1901–1904.

Jonas, H., 1979, *Le principe responsabilité: une éthique pour la civilisation technologique*, Paris: Editions du Cerf.

Levinas, E., 1961, *Totalité et infini. Essai sur l'extériorité*, Paris: Livre de Poche, Biblio-Essais, 1990.

Levinas, E., 1972, *Humanisme de l'autre homme*, Paris: Le Livre de Poche, Biblio Essais, 1987.

Nozick, R., 1974, *Anarchy, State and Utopia*, New York: Basic Books.

Ricoeur, P., 1960, *Philosophie de la volonté 2, Finitude et culpabilité, l'homme faillible*, Paris: Aubier.

Ricoeur, P., 1990, *Soi-même comme un autre*, Paris: Le Seuil.

Ricoeur, P., 2004, *Parcours de la reconnaissance*, Paris: Stock.

Schoeck, H., 1995, *L'envie. Une histoire du mal*, Paris: Les Belles Lettres.

Sen, A.K., 1993, *Ethique et économie*, Paris: PUF.

Index

theory of development 10, 20n3
Theory of Moral Sentiments, The
(Smith) 72, 82n5
time 37, 39–43, 64
Tolstoï, L. 38
totalitarianism 95
Totalité et infini (Levinas) 94
totality 38–39
transfers 99; state 63–64; *see also*
inter-living transfers; *inter vivos*
transfers

universality/universal norms 3, 8, 13,
24, 29–30, 34
utilitarianism 22, 48, 94, 99

Vacher de Lapouge, G. 30
Veblen, T. 5n3, 28, 29, 44n2

veil of ignorance (Rawls) 52, 71
virtue 99
Voltaire 92
Von Mises, L. 29, 30, 31
vulnerability 2, 5, 9, 57–66, 99;
anti-poverty policy and 59;
bioethics 59; definition 58–59;
human and social 58; responsibility
and 61–63; sustainable
development and 59

Walras, L. 35
Watsuji, T. 18–19
Weber, F. 5n4
Weber, M. 25, 47, 82n6
well-being, suffering and 68–72
West Africa 17–18
World Bank 16, 29, 57

Printed in the United States
by Baker & Taylor Publisher Services